IN SEARCH OF TRUTH

Five Stress-Free Steps to Discover Who You Are, Where You're Going, and How to Get There

Jacob Kashiwagi, Ph.D.

Cover design by Jonas Beer

Special Thanks to:
LogoMakr.com – Provider of graphics used in tables and figures
Jake A. Gunnoe, Nguyen Le, & David G. Krassa - Editing and formatting

The views expressed in this report are based solely on the independent research performed by the author. This publication does not necessarily represent the views of any of the partners or participating groups mentioned in this research.

Jacob Shizuo Kashiwagi
Connect with me at www.LinkedIn.com/in/JacobKashiwagi

Printed first in the United States of America

First Edition Fall 2018
KSM, Inc.

ISBN-13 978-0-9985836-2-4

CONTENTS

Thanks for purchasing
In Search of Truth!

Get a free copy of our eBook here: LeadAZ.org/Truth

Why Search for Truth

Author's Note

ver since I can remember, I have been on a quest. In search of something. As I have matured, the purpose of the quest has changed many times. When I was younger, the purpose tended to be shortsighted and often fleeting, sometimes even ridiculous and unrealistic. In the morning, it could be trying to steal a piece of gum from the pantry. In the afternoon, it could be trying to defeat the Decepticons from taking over the world. At the age of six, I debated with my friend what happens after we die. At the time, this might have caused my parents some consternation, as my father was on tour with the U.S. Air Force, and we were living in Saudi Arabia where it was against the law to talk about religion. At the age of thirteen, my math teacher asked us: "If you could have one wish, what would it be?" I responded, "To be a god." Suffice it to say, Mr. McWilliams never looked at me the same again.

The dilemma with the purpose of life always comes down to sustainability. Everyone wants to be happy, but we want to be happy forever. Being happy for one moment is not good enough if you are miserable the rest of your life. Thus, the purpose becomes, "How do you obtain happiness and keep it?" To do this you have to ensure fear, stress, and worry will never occur. Of course, you do not want to think about this too much or the thinking will increase your stress. Therefore, you must find a dominant answer. That answer for me was perfection. If you are perfect, and if you know everything, then nothing can make you fear, stress, or worry. In other words, you would be a god. Perfection in my mind equates to efficiency, productivity, success, understanding, and happiness. Someone who knows everything will understand why everything works. The more someone understands, the better they will perform, the faster they will be able to do things, the more efficiently they will be able to work. A perfect person no longer worries about having a job, money, or anything they desire that they know how to obtain. Someone who understands will also be able to maintain their youth and health longer. Thus, they are happy not just for a moment, but forever.

This quest for perfection brought many questions to my mind. The first being, "Why am I the only one with such a drive to know and understand what is going on?" I remember arguing with my religious leader at the age of twelve, telling him that if God made me, he also predestined my entire life, and for me to have free will, which my religion claimed I had, I could not have been made by God. After our conversation, I realized that my religious leader did not know how to answer my questions and did not care to know, which is when I realized not all people had a desire to know. In fact, most people do not.

In high school, I joined a lot of student clubs. Two of them that made an impact on me were Speech and Debate and Model United Nations. While most people went into those clubs to further their careers and gain experience in public speaking and politics, I went into them to figure out life. I found that Lincoln Douglas debating gave me a perfect platform to determine what principles were correct and which ones were not. I found it amazing that most people did not care to know the truth; they just cared about winning or socializing.

Eventually, I did find people who were on a quest just like me. People with an innate desire to know and understand life. Those are the people for whom I wrote this book, the ones who are seeking perfection, who are not satisfied with being happy for just one moment.

Over the history of humankind, society has encountered difficulties with the process of learning. During humankind's development, the first issue was trying to understand how things worked (the process of discovering). This was solved through the scientific method and trial and error. This led to the second issue: as we learned how to discover, we found the information and the understanding we were looking for, but we didn't know how to make the information easily accessible. When I was young, the answers to all my questions were always somewhere, I just didn't know where to find them or who to ask. This was solved by teachers and the education system and, eventually, the internet. Now that we have lots of information and everyone has access to it, we have encountered the unique problem of discovering which information is accurate and relevant to what we want. Google realized this, and it capitalized on being able to sort information based upon who we are and what we want, but we still have an issue with understanding which information is accurate and most aligned with reality. This has recently been referred to as the "fake news" phenomenon.

In the science realm, for example, there are many people who have ideas and explanations that do not follow the laws of physics. There are some mathematical principles that also could be called into question. And then there are the common existential questions, such as "Does God exist?" "Do we exist after we die?" and "How did we come into being?" Millions of people claim to have the answers for them, but few have proof. To solve this problem, some people decide to make this an individual quest and seek their own answers. However, this only works for so long. There is only so much time in the day, and no one will ever have enough time to verify all the information out there to learn for themselves. Thus, with our limited understanding, how can anyone know what reality is?

This question fueled my quest to find the truth, to understand everything, and in doing so, to become perfect.

Introduction

Unlocking the Truth

College is where my journey toward finding the truth began. During my experience at Arizona State University, I became involved with a construction leadership group, led by Professor William W. Badger. Dr. Badger was old enough at the time to have served on both my father's dissertation committee and my own. Dr. Badger's only rule was that he had no rules. This allowed me freedom in my academic career to shape my research and education into what I wanted. Dr. Badger and my father, who was also a professor at ASU, helped me realize the keys to finding truth.

I like to explain this using a parable I call the "The Bank Robber":

There once was a skilled bank robber who attempted to rob the largest and most secure safe in the city. Armed with the most advanced tools and techniques, he snuck into the bank and attempted to break into the vault. However, his confidence began to wane as hours went by and he was still unable to open it. In his despair, he accidently leans against the handle, and to his surprise, the safe door opened. In amazement, he began to realize that the safe was never locked; he just had to turn the handle.

This is much like finding the truth. Society feels that to find the truth, you need a great amount of expertise, understanding, and in many cases, technologically advanced tools, equipment, and labs to conduct experiments. They think that truth is locked away so only the most intelligent can access it. They think that it would be impossible for something so valuable to be left unlocked and in the open for anyone to take. This is far from the case. In reality, the door to truth has never been locked. It takes very little effort to access; you just have to turn the handle. In the meantime, the rest of society is hurrying and scurrying to and fro, doing this and that, looking at this place and that place, only to be disappointed and frustrated at the result.

To find the truth, one must look at life differently. He or she must have a desire to know. In the parable, the robber believed that no one would ever leave the bank vault unlocked. Hence, although it was the easiest solution to turn the handle, in his mind, it wasn't even an option. This is very similar to many things we do in life. The truth is right in front of us, but instead of opening our eyes, we have to go through tremendous effort trying to find it with our eyes closed, because of our preconceived notions.

In 1962, Bob Dylan composed the song *Blowin' in the Wind*. In 2004, Rolling Stone magazine identified it as one of the greatest songs of all times (Rolling Stone, 2011). The song presents Dylan's realization that truth is everywhere, and those who stop to observe and look for it will find it. In Dylan's own words, "There ain't too much I can say about this song except that the answer is blowing in the wind. It ain't in no book or movie or TV show or discussion group.... Too many of these hip people are telling me where the answer is but oh I won't believe that. I still say it's in the wind and just like a restless piece of paper it's got to come down some... But the only trouble is that no one picks up the answer when it comes down so not too many people get to see and know . . . and then it flies away...." (Gray, 2006). The lyrics of the last two verses are as follows:

How many years can a mountain exist
Before it's washed to the sea?
Yes, 'n' how many years can some people exist
Before they're allowed to be free?
Yes, 'n' how many times can a man turn his head
Pretending he just doesn't see?
The answer, my friend, is blowin' in the wind
The answer is blowin' in the wind
How many times must a man look up
Before he can see the sky?
Yes, 'n' how many ears must one man have
Before he can hear people cry?
Yes, 'n' how many deaths will it take till he knows
That too many people have died?
The answer, my friend, is blowin' in the wind
The answer is blowin' in the wind.

It is not difficult to find the truth; it is all around us. No one can hide it or stop you from finding it because it is everywhere. All it takes is someone to look at life the right way to see it.

Being the fourth of eight children, I have seen numerous examples of this in my own life. Out of the eight kids, for example, only two of us did not finish college. I have watched some of my siblings go through college the traditional way. Trying to figure it out on their own. Spending lots of time researching their options, studying, and participating in every activity to not miss an opportunity, stressing and worrying the entire time. I have seen other siblings spend relatively no time on the process. Their secret? They found someone who had been through the experience before, then they let them plan their entire college career, and they just followed the plan. They took the right classes, minimized their work, maximized their learning, and minimized their stress and worrying. In the meantime, they relaxed and enjoyed the experience.

During my childhood, I was the sibling who had to figure it out on my own. I was the one who took the difficult way. Why? I just didn't know. I was the first son to receive a bachelor's degree, and first child to get a Ph.D. I had no clue what I was doing, and it didn't dawn on me that I should have been looking for someone who had done it already. I didn't realize that you don't need to exhort a great amount of effort to be successful. After a while, I asked myself, "What am I doing? I spend all this effort, I go through all this pain, I do all these things I don't want to do, and in the end, I don't learn anything." I might not be the smartest person, but it does not take a genius to realize something had to change.

In my search, I have found five keys to unlocking the truth, or turning the handle:

> Key 1: Knowing That You Don't Know
> Key 2: No Exceptions
> Key 3: Power of Observation
> Key 4: Utilizing Expertise
> Key 5: Taking the Extreme

Each key can unlock the truth. However, as with life, sometimes you may need multiple keys to access something so valuable. Using all of the keys gives a person tremendous capability to find, identify, and observe any truth. It is important to remember that finding truth is not like buying a tool; when you buy a drill, you can immediately start drilling holes and then put it away when you are done. Finding the truth is more like learning how to dance or learning martial arts. It is not something that you can use and then put away. It is something that will change how you live. When you learn to dance, your posture will change, and your rhythm will improve. It will change how you walk, how you listen to music, what music you like, how you feel when you listen to music, and what thoughts come into your mind when you hear songs. However, it takes time to learn to dance—just as it takes time to find the truth. The application into your life might not come all at once, but with these keys, the truth will be possible to find.

I have a small statue of a Hindu God in my office. It was given to me by an Indian graduate student I worked with. It represents Shiva. I came to learn that Shiva is not only the God of creation, but also that of destruction. I found this odd that the Hindu's believe that one God is over two seemingly opposite things. However, the idea made sense when explained to me. It is impossible to make something out of nothing. Hence, to create something new in the universe, it must always have come from something that was already there. Thus, destruction is the first step in creation. This is also the same with finding truth. Your mind is full of ideas. Most of them are probably incorrect. If you are to make room for correct principles, you will have to be willing to destroy or cast out the inaccurate ones. Destruction is never a happy thing; it is difficult to go through. Those who have been through it realize that.

To find the truth, one must be willing, and capable, of opening their life and letting go of anything and everything. Because the mind shapes all that we do, nothing is safe. The mind affects all the aspects of our life, including our career, religion, family, relationships, and hobbies.

In this book, truth and reality are synonymous. The goal of finding truth is the goal of learning to identify and accept reality. Due to society developing a culture of opinions and acceptance, there are many thoughts and ideas of what reality is. Many people forget that even though everyone sees life differently, it doesn't mean that everyone's view of life is true and accurate. Just because something is said on the news doesn't mean it is correct. When someone knows the truth, it simplifies life greatly. Many concepts are only confusing because we don't know.

Here are some examples:

1. Religion – God either exists or does not exist. If we knew which one it was, then it would eliminate many religious thoughts and sects.
2. Cancer treatment – If we knew the "cause" of cancer, many thoughts on cancer and how it is treated would disappear.
3. Dieting – Either sugar and meat cause disease and cancer, or they do not. If we knew this, many ideas, legislation, and diets would cease to be options.

In other words, there is a reality, and then there is people's perception of reality. Common ideas wouldn't have any validity if everyone knew the truth. The more information and understanding you have, the less you listen to most people's opinions, and the more you only listen to people who know.

In sports, for example, it never ceases to amaze me how much airtime some commentators spend on speculating. They talk about why they *think* what is happening is actually happening, and what they *think* will ultimately happen. If only the truth or reality was spoken, it would eliminate 90 percent of what they say.

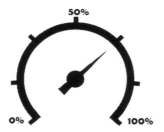

Figure 1: The Truth Meter

When you look at everything in life on a scale of information gauged by accuracy, it helps you see what it takes to embrace the truth (Figure 1). As I mentioned, everything is either correct or it's incorrect. If someone knew everything in the world with complete accuracy, they would have 100 percent truth. This person would be able to know how the flapping wings of a bee in Africa affect the weather in Alaska. Even though people can't know everything, we can still use this scale to determine who knows *more* or, who has a *more accurate* perception of reality.

Let's go through a little exercise to grasp the impact. First, let's think of organizations and groups that people belong to. This could be religious groups like Christianity, Buddhism, and Atheism. It could also be education groups like universities, think tanks, and vocation schools. There are also political and social groups, such as sports teams, fan clubs, social media groups, political affiliations, and cultural groups. If you took away the names of these organizations (religious, education, and social), how would you tell them apart? Could you tell *any* of them apart? The answer is yes. You could tell them apart based upon their view of reality.

When it comes down to it, every organization is trying to describe their perception of reality. Educational organizations are typically seen as more scientific and closer to reality. However, religious organizations are also teaching their view of reality. They focus more on what they think will happen after death and subjects that we have very little empirical evidence on, so this is seen as more subjective and not as scientific. Then you have political and social groups, who also are trying to spread their view of reality and what they think is important to focus on or the most accurate way to run society.

Knowing that these organizations are teaching different ideas of reality, two questions come to mind:

1. Do any of these organizations have the same perception?
2. Is there only one accurate way to view the truth?

Do any of these organizations have the same perception?
No. If two organizations had the exact same perspective, they would not be two different organizations. Yes, some religions might be similar, but even if they differ in their opinion or belief in one minor idea or action, they will be different. This is seen in many

Christian religions. They all believe that Jesus Christ is their Savior, but when you get into the details of who he is, his story, the interpretation of the scriptures, or how to worship him, you find that they differ from one church to the other. In fact, many times even in the same church, people have different beliefs and interpretations of the scriptures.

Is there only one accurate way to view the truth?

Yes. Observation tells us that people with more information have a more accurate way to view reality. Thus, the organization, or person, with the most amount of information will have the most accurate view of reality. There can only be one organization that knows 100 percent of the truth, and if that organization existed, it would have a 100 percent accurate view of reality.

In other words, there is only *one* truth. What does this mean? What is the impact of there being only one truth? It means although there are many people teaching different ideas, only one idea is accurate. Although there are multiple organizations in the world, only one will have the most accurate view of reality. "One truth" does not mean "the best truth," or the one that works for everybody. It just means the most accurate or real. All ideas have a degree of accuracy to them, but there is only one view that is 100 percent accurate. This conclusion has some life-changing implications:

1. From an information scale, everything about you is related. Your religion, friends, political views, hobbies, occupation, etc. Everything that you do and think identifies how much information you understand.
2. People who have more information do similar things; they belong to groups, support things, and have the same thoughts and ideas as each other.
3. If you want to know the truth, you will have to change many of your ideas... unless you already have 100 percent information.

This means that if you are looking for the truth, you will have to give up some deep-seated religious beliefs, political views, family traditions, or academic ideas. To "search for truth" is another way of saying, "eliminating everything that is inaccurate in your mind." Anyone who has tried to give up an inaccurate thought knows it is the most difficult thing to do in the world. Hopefully these five keys will make it easier for you to do that in your quest to turn that handle and unlock the truth.

Key #1:

Knowing That You Don't Know

Many of the principles in this book directly oppose what society considers to be common knowledge. It's important to recognize that most ideas in society are widely accepted because of bias, and not reason. Society values position and authority above all else. Therefore, if a supposed "expert" (scientist, historian, professor, etc.) makes a claim, people are more likely to assume it's true. As a research professor at a public university, I have witnessed this first hand. Academic journals tend to publish research that promote their image or authority instead proliferating controversial, but logical works.

One of the characteristics of someone who thinks they know something is that they fabricate things. This is how all incorrect ideas begin. Many people have approached me asking about inaccurate ideas that a respected individual taught them to be true. Upon hearing that the idea is inaccurate, they immediately proclaim, "Why would they teach us an idea that does not have some sort of evidence supporting it? Why would they just make it up?" My response is always the same: "They don't know they are making it up. Subconsciously, even educated people make up false ideas and insist that they're fact."

Most often, when someone makes something up, they are ignorant of what they are doing. Everyone does it. Even I do it. One time, a new girl joined us for racquetball. My brother asked me who she was. I told him her name was Stacy, which was incorrect. Her name was Bella. I didn't mean to lie to him; my mind at that moment just thought her name was Stacy. Where did that name come from? I made it up. It is difficult to realize when you don't really know.

Try testing this idea on yourself by answering this question: What happens when people die? You probably had many thoughts come into your mind. If you are honest, you made up most of those ideas. In other words, they are not based on evidence or experience.

This happens quite frequently for most people. A good way to catch yourself making up something is by asking yourself why you believe something, why you think the way you do, and how you know it is accurate. This is difficult for most people, because most people make up many things. In fact, it is so difficult, that most people do not want to know the truth. When you find out how many people "most" is, it can get depressing. However, there are some people who do want to know the truth. There are many things a person can want, but the truth is the pinnacle of all desire. I didn't realize this until I got older.

Throughout history, there have been individuals who have changed the incorrect notions of society. Christopher Columbus eliminated the idea that the world was flat. William Wilberforce started a movement to help Britain see that no man should be a slave. They were both able to realize one thing: they had to know what they did not know. They had to overcome the prejudices and biased opinions of society, their friends, and mentors. They had to ask themselves why people believed the world was flat, or why people thought some people deserve to be treated better than others. Is it based upon evidence and reality?

On a lighter note, consider Michael Jackson, who created a new dimension for dancing that still has people amazed today. Jackson realized that he and society didn't know all the ways to dance. He had to continually learn to find new ways to express himself. It allowed him to experiment, to learn from others, and eventually identify ways to dance that no one else thought of.

No one understood this idea more than the Greek philosopher Socrates. His ability to use common sense and logic to challenge societal norms has left a lasting impact on the advancement of science and the development of society. His greatest strength was he knew that he knew nothing. The story goes:

> *"Apollo, the god of Delphi, had declared him (Socrates) to be the wisest human being, but at the end of a long pilgrimage searching for the meaning of the oracle and in the fulfillment of his divine mission, he reaches the conclusion that he is indeed the wisest among all human beings because he knows that he knows little or nothing. Other people, blinded by their ill-founded opinions and their arrogance, do not even know that they know nothing..."*
> *(Plato. et al., 2010).*

Recognizing his ignorance, Socrates knew what he did not know. It allowed him to be open to truth and understanding that many were not. One example is Socrates's ability to deal with death:

> *"For all anyone knows, death might even be the greatest of goods to man, but people fear it as if they knew it was the greatest of evils. But is not this the most disgraceful ignorance, supposing one knows what one does not know? I, gentlemen, perhaps differ in this matter, too, from other men, and if I were to say that I am wiser than they, it would be in this, that not knowing very much about what is in Hades, I do not think I know....."*

To Socrates, one of the greatest obstacles to learning is the presumption that you know when you do not:

> *"...the good craftsmen, just as the good poets, seemed to me to have the same failing. Because he performs his craft well, each believed he is wisest about the other most important things. And this error of theirs obscured their wisdom, so that I asked myself on behalf of the oracle, whether I should prefer to be thus as I am, being neither wise with respect to their wisdom nor ignorant with respect to their ignorance, or to have both things that they have.*

I then answered myself and the oracle that it would be better for me to be as I am."

A person who knows what they do not know will keep their mind open, ask questions, and verify information. It is amazing how many false ideas could be quickly discarded today by just doing a simple google search. Being open, however, does not mean to give every idea you come across the same amount of credibility and attention. An open mind indicates that a person is willing to consider ideas that are foreign or opposed to their usual way of thinking if evidence is presented to support a change. This means that a person's openness, credence, and interest to an idea will be directly correlated with the level of evidence that is presented to provide support for the idea. In the case where there is an overwhelming amount of evidence presented, an open mind will be more accepting of the idea. As the level of evidence decreases, the idea is more likely to be dismissed, ignored, or cast off as incorrect. An open mind does not determine reality (i.e., accept or reject ideas) by familiarity, relationship, or hearsay, but by the level of evidence and information presented on the idea.

In short, the ability to realize when one is accepting or rejecting an idea based off valid information or pre-supposed ideas is the ability to know when one does not know.

Most people go through life thinking that they know everything, when in fact they know very little. In fact, many times a person will even have an incorrect perception of what they themselves are thinking and desiring.

For example, take a child telling their parent that the only thing they want to eat is candy. The question is, "Is that really all the child wants to eat?" The obvious answer is no. How do we know? Because eating candy will eventually cause the child's body to deteriorate. He then would not be able to think right, and he would be in constant pain. The child is not intelligent enough to realize eating nothing but candy is equivalent to asking to die a slow and very painful death. The child really does not want to eat only candy; he is explaining that he likes the taste of candy and would prefer to eat it above anything else. The child is asking for one thing, but really wanting something else. However, because the child is ignorant of what he does not know, he asks to eat only candy.

The above example is not only applicable to children, but to adults as well. The child represents a person who is ignorant and not as developed in their understanding. The more ignorant a person is, the more they do not know what they are thinking. They will say one thing, but mean something else, oblivious to what they desire or are thinking. For example, many people wish and believe that they want to win the lottery or inherit a large amount of money. However, they don't realize that when you have a large amount of money, you will need to spend time taking care of it, becoming educated in the financial world, finding honest people to deal with and help you with the money, spend time and effort dealing with people who want your money, etc. If they knew that most people who win the lottery become less happy and usually lose all their money after 10 years, they might realize they don't really want a lot of money. On the other hand, when someone is intelligent, they are quick to realize that they might not know what would be best for them and are more satisfied with their situation in life and are more apt to listen to older and wiser people.

Mozart is a good example of this. Although Mozart was one of the most talented prodigies in music, he seemed to realize that there was still a lot he needed to learn. Mozart spent a tremendous amount of time learning from other talented and successful musicians of his time. Mozart is one of the most well-trained musicians to ever have lived. One of his teachers was a musician named Giovanni Battista Martini from Italy. He was known for his understanding and skill in counterpoint. Mozart met him when Giovanni was in his 60s, and he went through intense counterpoint exercises with Giovanni and the most formal version of counterpoint: the fugue. All his life Mozart would learn from others, incorporating their ideas and techniques into his own compositions (Sadie, 2017).

Since most people don't know that they don't know, there have been many ideas that have been taught as truth or reality that are incorrect. Even people who seem to have excelled to the highest levels of their expertise have been found to support concepts that have been proven to be false. One of the greatest difficulties in life is sifting out the incorrect ideas.

Knowing what you don't know is a key attribute of life. This is what allows some people to learn quicker, understand others better, and have a greater vision. There is a misconception today that to be a successful individual, one must have superior talent or a high intellect. When, in fact, it only requires someone who can admit when something does not make sense.

Albert Einstein changed the world with a simple idea that everyone observed every day: light takes time to travel and has a set speed. Thus, our perception of everything is relative. For example, the closer you are to a lightning strike, the sooner you will see it. As simple as it seems, it took a struggling student to challenge an age-old law (Newton's law of absolute time) that even the most educated physics professors in the world followed blindly at the time.

Key #1: Summary

The first key to finding truth is recognizing that you don't know. Those who recognize they don't know do the following:

1. Ask themselves why they believe an idea is correct. If it is not supported by evidence, they realize that it could be wrong.
2. The more an idea is supported by facts when presented to them, the more credence they give to the idea, regardless of if it is against what they believe.
3. They seek out intelligent and skilled people to listen to and learn from.

By doing the above three things, even for a week, you will be able to correct many false ideas that you have in your mind. You will be able to realize what you don't know. The biggest advantage in knowing what you don't know is that it allows you to change and improve.

When you can't recognize that you don't know, you can't change. Instead, you continue living life with the same incorrect practices and beliefs. The truth is only available to people who are willing to make room for it. Before you can unlock the truth, you must first recognize the need for it in your own life.

Key #2:
No Exceptions

Recently, I had the opportunity to visit my childhood neighborhood. I passed by our old rental house and my elementary school, and I drove through the streets that I used to spend my summer days exploring. The world seemed like such an amazing place back then. I remember how I would marvel at the size of the houses and the infrastructure of the community. To me, our quarter-mile block seemed like an entire universe. Since then, I have changed neighborhoods many times and I have had the opportunity to travel the world.

An interesting thing occurred to me as I walked my old stomping grounds: everything looked different. Somehow, in twenty years, the neighborhood changed. It shrunk. The mystery and excitement of walking down the street had disappeared. It made me stop and think about what happened. My first impression was, "This neighborhood sure has changed." However, reality quickly came back to me, and I realized the neighborhood had not changed, I had changed! The houses were the same, the streets were the same size, even the elementary school had not had any major infrastructure changes. It was the exact same neighborhood, but it was a different me. This made me realize the incorrect conclusion that most people come to in life: because our perspective of reality is changing as we acquire more information, we assume that reality is always changing, but it is not. This is the lesson we must learn in finding the truth. Reality does not change. If we see or experience something in life that doesn't make sense or is not what we have seen in the past, this tells us that we are wrong, not reality. It tells us that we are missing something in life and that we need to observe more.

To understand Key #2, we must first identify what reality is. Reality is made of two forms of information: natural laws and conditions.

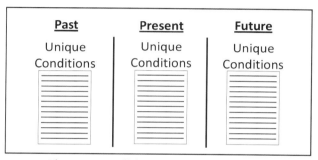

Figure 2: Conditions Diagram (D. Kashiwagi, 2018)

At any given point in time a person can take a snapshot of life and record various observations regarding that moment. Those observations might include position, time, objects, people, ideas, and so on. These observations are known as conditions. As time changes, the conditions will also change. For each person, their conditions will always be unique because no two people can be in the same place at the same time. Reality is defined when someone accurately identifies what the unique conditions are or what they will be.

The next key component to reality is natural laws. Natural laws are rules that all conditions in life are governed by. They are patterns that enable us to predict how conditions change. Natural laws are what relate the past conditions to the future conditions. They determine what is possible. Natural laws are what enable society to learn and progress over time. They create consistency in life.

The opposite of natural laws is randomness and chance, which suggest events, people, and materials do not follow a pattern or happen for a reason. Randomness suggests that one day a person can be walking down the street and start floating, and the next minute they would fall to the ground. Without the law of gravity, nothing is predictable; anything could happen. In a world of chance and randomness, there is no progress. You could be planting tomato seeds one day, and the next thing you know, you have bushels of corn in your field. There is no ability to plan or to develop when everything is random.

We see this every day in life. Those who understand more can anticipate what will happen beforehand and begin to plan for it. Those who understand less seem to think things are more random and are unable to plan for it. Take studying for a high school or college exam. Those who understand the class seem to know what they should study and will be better prepared for exams. Those who don't understand seem to get confused and feel like the teacher could put anything on the exam. They find it difficult to prepare for it and find themselves not ready for it.

Natural laws and randomness are extreme opposites. Usually, people do not believe extremes; they believe something in the middle. People believe that natural laws exist, but they also believe that there are things in life that do not abide by natural laws that are random. For example, when applying for a job, people who are more qualified and have worked harder are often hired. However, many believe that there are exceptions. Sometimes when applying for a job, people could get "lucky" and, by chance, get a job that they were not the best qualified for. This is probably one of the major ideas that prevents people from understanding reality and finding the truth: the belief that there are exceptions in life or to natural laws.

The only reason people believe in chance and randomness (or exceptions) is because they just don't have enough information and either do not understand enough natural laws or accurately understand what a natural law is. In every case throughout time where we have been able to collect and perceive more information, it has always proven that something once thought random was something explainable and went according to natural law. The only things that we think are random are things we do not have enough information about. Consider the following examples:

1. People used to believe that flies spontaneously generated from rotting meat until Francesco Redi proved it wrong.
2. It was common knowledge that evil spirits would randomly kill pregnant women, until Ignaz Semmelweis discovered that doctors were transferring bacteria when they washed their hands (Davis, 2015).
3. Gambling was thought to be an unpredictable recreation until computers paved the way to create advanced prediction models.

Natural laws include physical phenomena such as the law of gravity or the laws of thermodynamics. However, there are also laws that relate to human action. These are more difficult to identify, as the human body and mind are harder to observe, but there are many obvious human laws. As children age, they grow in stature and maturity. As we get old, our bodies become weak. Tragedy causes mental instability. Practice leads to improved skill. When someone says, "We need to talk" they are really saying, "You need to listen." The self-help book industry is fueled by authors trying to describe different laws of human nature.

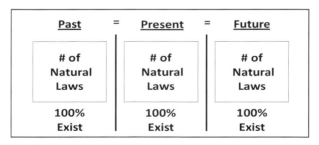

Figure 3: Number of Natural Laws (D. Kashiwagi, 2018)

Hence, whenever someone accurately identifies a pattern in life, such as the law of gravity or human attention, they identify a part of reality. Thus, whenever someone accurately identifies a natural law or conditions (whether past, present, or future), they identify truth. In other words, "Truth are things as they are, as they were, and as they are to come," and it never changes.

When we are looking specifically at natural laws, it is important to note that when something is true, then there can be no exceptions. In 2016, real estate billionaire Donald Trump was elected president despite his lack of political experience and refinement. During the primary elections, analysts insisted that there was no way Trump could win the presidential nomination for the party. When he beat the odds, was nominated, and was eventually elected president, they proposed that it was an anomaly. Thus, Trump was an exception. The thought never occurred to them that maybe their political models and tools were inaccurate.

Exceptions are a bad habit that society has slowly developed due to our inability to know everything. You find exceptions to the rules all the time only because you do not fully understand the rule or natural law. Take the law of gravity, for example. Does it work everywhere? Many people will answer that it doesn't. Why? The common answer is because in outer space you float and do not fall. However, this is not an exception, this is due to people's misunderstanding of the definition of the law of gravity. The law of gravity is a mathematical equation that identifies that mass attracts mass. It considers the size of the mass and the distance of one mass to another mass. Hence, when you only have one mass, the law of gravity identifies that you will not be drawn anywhere, you will float.

Let's go back to the example about applying for a job. Many think the law is that the quality of your resume and your qualifications is how you obtain jobs. Thus, they believe in exceptions to the law as they see other people, based upon relationships or social status, obtain a job position. In reality, there is no exception. Jobs are not obtained solely upon qualifications; they never were. In fact, many jobs are obtained through a relationship or connection with someone who is not even in the same industry or company.

There are many inaccurate ideas that are taught and believed in society. We know this just by looking at how many exceptions we find in ideas said to be "natural law." Children quickly pick up on this from when they are young, as they find out their parents have taught them ideas and requirements of life that don't make sense and do not follow reality. Children are taught that they must have good grades to be successful, and then they find out about Bill Gates, Steve Jobs, Albert Einstein, and others who were very successful, yet did not get good grades or did not finish high school or college (Gillet, 2015).

Due to the internet and easy access to information, it does not take long for us to realize that many things people say have exceptions or, in other words, are inaccurate. Most of the time, it does not hurt us too much to believe in "false laws," like the homemade remedies to illness or the placebo rituals we do that help us perform better only because we think they are doing something. We could keep many of these inaccurate ideas in our head and still not have them affect our lives very much. However, there are some false laws that do have a drastic impact on life and our ability to advance.

Isaac Newton, for example, in discovering the laws of physics, identified an idea called "absolute time." This law states that it doesn't matter where you are, everything happens at the same time. In other words, light does not take time to travel. Thus, if you have two people, one closer to and one farther away from a lightning strike, absolute time says they will see the bolt at the same time. This idea of "absolute time" stopped many of the advancements in technology. It changed the laws of physics to aid in the development of much of the technology we have today, such as global positioning systems and nuclear technology. However, the greatest minds of physics believed the idea of "absolute time" for more than two hundred years. It wasn't until Albert Einstein came around in the 1800s that this idea was corrected (Albert Einstein – Biographical, 2014). Today, computers, cell phones, and satellites all operate based on the idea that light takes time to travel.

It is important to note that there is a difference between an exception and an inaccurate law. There is also a difference between an exception and something that can't be explained. Technically, in science, we have never found a real verified exception. We have found many inaccurate laws, but no exceptions. A real exception would be like saying the law is 1+1=2, but an exception to that rule would be if one time 1+1=3. Over time, science has found that the more information we obtain on any subject, the more we find there are no exceptions to the law.

Due to a lack of information on many aspects of the universe, there are several areas that we do not understand, and it leads people to often mistake an exception to the rule for a lack of understanding or inaccurate law. Religion, for example, is a big promoter of exceptions. In religious terms, an exception is called a miracle. A miracle is something that can't be explained, something that goes against natural law. It is something thought to be magic. The idea of miracles is one reason why science does not like religion. But, ironically, academia and science also believe in "miracles" or exceptions. When taking mathematics and physics, they will teach students a concept, but most of the class time is spent on understanding all the exceptions to the concept. Even Stephen Hawking teaches of "singularities," points in space where natural laws don't exist, places where anything can happen. Or, in other words: miracles and magic (Hawking, 1942).

The truth never changes. Our own views and perceptions might change as time goes on. However, when something is true, it will never stop being true. I might have viewed life differently when I was three feet tall, weighed fifty pounds, and had seen so few neighborhoods in my seven years of existence, but that didn't change the community from what it actually was: a quarter-mile, middle class neighborhood.

People are imperfect; we know very little on the truth scale (closer to 0 percent than to 100 percent). Since people are imperfect, we are raised to depend on exceptions. Everyone knows the common axiom, "Rules are meant to be broken." This might be true about human-made rules, but people mistakenly believe that this is also true for natural laws. This leads people to believe that absolute truth does not exist.

In the 1980s, Edwards Deming, a statistician, was called upon by automobile manufacturers to help them identify their issues and increase their efficiency. Deming realized that the manufacturers were having difficulties fixing their problems, because they did not understand natural laws and believed in exceptions (Andrews, 1994).

Deming realized manufacturers thought there were two reasons for issues in manufacturing: some are due to special causes, and others are due to common causes. Special causes are the result of something out of the ordinary occurring, or what many would label as an exception. Common causes are the result of the laws of successful business practices not being followed, meaning the company needs to adjust the way it does business.

For example, say there are three workers whose jobs are to make peanut butter and jelly sandwiches. After watching the three employees, you find that one of the employees is making fifteen percent less sandwiches a day than the other two. Many employers would jump to the conclusion that this is a special cause, or an exception, created by the poor performance of that employee. However, on further investigation, it is determined that one employee's work station is farther from the peanut butter and jelly supply than the workstations of the other two employees. The additional amount of time it takes for that employee to transport the peanut butter and jelly to his work station decreases the amount of time he has to make the sandwiches by fifteen percent. The real cause of the poor performance is not due to the employee, it is because of the position of the workstation.

Most issues that occur in organizations are often attributed to special causes, meaning an issue is due to a certain employee, an abnormal condition, or an accident. Deming, however, found that all the issues he looked at were due to a common cause, or a flaw in the system. This was Deming's way of telling people that there were no exceptions. Natural laws must be followed. So, when there is an issue, it is not an exception; there is a cause or reason behind the occurrence. In other words, people do not realize it, but their perception of reality is flawed. And if they keep following the same ideas, the issue will happen again.

Deming understood the natural laws of business and industry, but his attempts to teach them to American automobile manufactures ended in failure. Deming had to travel to the other side of the world before anyone listened to him. He was well-received in Japan. Since the U.S. did not heed Deming's advice, they paid for it down the road, which should have been no surprise to anyone. Whenever we ignore natural laws, we eventually pay the price.

Less than thirty years later the world realized the wisdom of Deming's counsel. In 2009, after the collapse of the financial industry, many of the U.S. auto manufacturers began filing for bankruptcy (Figure 4). Several of them claimed that the disaster was unforeseeable. On the other hand, the Japanese auto manufacturers that took Deming's advice were not only financially stable, they now had a reputation that helped them capture a greater share of the U.S. automobile buyers.

Figure 4: U.S. Vehicle Sales Market Share 1961 to 2011

One of my students exercises with me every morning at the gym. A month after we started working out together, we were playing racquetball when he hit his knee trying to swing at the ball. At first, it seemed like he just bruised it. However, the pain would prevent him from playing racquetball for two months. It seemed like an "exception" or "special cause," an unlucky event. He never considered it was due to a common cause—the way he was living his life or how he was exercising. Three weeks after his knee pain did not go away, he sought my advice on how to fix it. I fortunately knew a good knee doctor who could help him. However, I took a moment to try to help him figure out a way to make sure he didn't hurt himself again. First, we made a list of characteristics that we could use to explain his life:

1. Extreme
2. Unaware of what is going on around him
3. Acts before he thinks
4. Does not know his limits
5. Does not ask for help
6. Lack of self-control

Then we looked at the last three months in his life and realized he'd had several health issues:

1. Burned his hands doing a pull-up contest.
2. Hurt his shoulder lifting weights.
3. Had gotten sick.
4. Hurt his knee playing racquetball.

As we wrote down the facts and processed the information, he realized the things that seemed to be random and by chance, supposed one-time events, were not so random. He knew he needed to change the way he lived.

Whether in your personal life or business, because the world is complex, it seems that things happen by chance; in other words, they do not follow natural law. Things can happen to you or others that are totally unrelated to who you are and what you deserve. However, if you think about it, we have observed the following:

1. Whenever we have more information on the event, the event always seems less random, and it always seems to follow natural laws and logic.
2. The more information we have on an event, the more we realize everything is related and relevant.
3. Whenever we have all the information on an event and we find an exception, we have always found that what we thought was the natural law was wrong.

It is difficult to understand the idea of no exceptions because we know so little on the truth meter. Exceptions make it easier for us to justify lacking information. We see this when someone gets sick even when they exercise and eat healthy, or when we see people who have been honest and hardworking get robbed of their money and efforts. We have become accustomed to say that life is unfair and sometimes doesn't follow natural law and logic. Since no one has 100 percent information and understanding, and because there are millions of variables to consider, it is impossible for one person to know the reason why everything happens in life. However, we find that every event in which we have a lot of information does happen for a reason and follows natural law.

When you realize that there are no exceptions in life, you will then begin to realize something that will simplify your life and greatly increase your understanding of it: not only does everything in life always follow the laws (nothing is random or by chance), but the laws will apply in every aspect of life. This means if you learn something at church and it is correct, then it should also apply to your work, relationships, and hobbies. Or if a father learned the best way to improve his family life and increase their bond together is by spending more time with his children and wife, and if this is an accurate natural law, then this concept should also work to improve his business team and bowling team's bond and performance.

Because there are no exceptions, when you identify an accurate natural law, then you identify something that can be applied to every area of your life. Natural laws become very valuable because of the impact they will have on all aspects of your life.

Key #2: Summary

Key #2 identifies that reality always follows natural law and that there are no exceptions in life. In other words, there is no such thing as chance or randomness. Thus, if you are searching for the truth, this key tells you to unlock it in the following ways:

1. Look for things that you believe are exceptions in life and gather more information on it.
2. Anything that is based on chance, randomness, or luck, is an inaccurate idea.
3. You can identify if something is true if it works in all aspects of your life.
4. The one thing people have the most information on is themselves. Identify who you are and trace back why things have happened in your life and what the causes were.

Since everything that happens in life is based upon reality (natural laws and conditions), one of the most important things a person can do in life to find truth is to observe reality. This leads to our third key.

Key #3:

Power of Observation

There is a story of a father who had a son going through a rough time in his life. One day the father had an idea to help his struggling son. He blindfolded his son and took him up a mountain onto a cliff. On the cliff he put his son's head behind a big rock and took off the blind fold. When he took off the blindfold, he asked the son, "What do you see?" The son responded, "A rock." The father then gently lifted the son's head to reveal a magnificent valley. As the son stood gazing at this amazing sight, the father asked the son, "How big does the rock look now?"

The ability to see the big picture, to understand the relative importance of events, things, and people, is critical to finding the truth. In fact, nothing will help you see your physical environment more accurately than opening your eyes and looking. This is the same for understanding reality. Nothing will help you more than opening your eyes. In other words, you must learn the power of observation.

I quickly learned this after getting married. It was then when I finally understood the famous Biblical words of Jesus Christ: "...they seeing see not; and hearing they hear not...." No one forewarned me that some people might say one thing but mean something totally different. How was I to know that when she asked, "Where is my cell phone?" she meant, "Please get up and look for my cell phone." Or when she asks me to cook dinner, she was expecting something edible. Or when she asks for advice, it really means, "I already know the answer, just listen to me." Yes, I finally learned the hard way that, to listen to your spouse is of great value, but to know what they want and what they mean without them having to explain it to you, is priceless. This is crucial to any happy relationship. So, the question then becomes, "How do you learn to read minds?"

By becoming an excellent observer. At the start of my marriage, I was given a lot of time to think and observe. Mainly because my wife would take thirty minutes longer to get ready each time we went out than we had time for. Luckily, I had a smartphone with Netflix on it. I watched all 121 episodes (six full seasons) of the Star Wars cartoon series *Clone Wars* while she was getting ready. While watching, I made a couple profound observations: first, this was not really a child's cartoon, and second, I should be doing something more productive with my time. However, one silver lining was a small clip from one of the episodes that helped me realize why so many people have a difficult time improving themselves and realizing who they are. In this clip, Yoda, the wise old master, has to gain immortality. To do this, he had to overcome his fear. The clip shows Yoda venturing onto an island where he finds his "evil self". The evil-self claims that Yoda doesn't like him anymore. Yoda claims that he does not recognize his evil self. A battle ensues in which Yoda eventually becomes weak and is about to succumb to his evil self. In his last effort to survive, he recognizes that this evil he is fighting is himself, which allows him to accept it and overcome it. The interesting thing about this story is that most people realize that to overcome, we must accept our weakness. However, most people do not understand that, in order to accept, we must first recognize. People have issues accepting themselves, because they don't even know who they are.

This reminds me of various foreign graduate students who have worked in my research group at ASU. I quickly realized that many of them were not raised with the same standards of hygiene that are expected in an American professional environment. I had to take many of them aside to explain that they need to shower regularly and should use deodorant. It is always a shock to them, because most did not realize their body odor was an issue. In fact, in some instances it took a little while to help the student figure out how to minimize their body odor. The first step to finding truth is the ability to recognize what it is, and that can only come through observation.

The issue with observation is that it must come from within the individual. It is not something that can be given to them. Reality is always around us. All the information is around us. The constraint is not that we don't have access to reality, the constraint is that we either don't want to or don't have the capability to open our eyes and see it. It is a natural law of life that people do not purposefully do things that are detrimental to themselves and others. They do them because they don't recognize that they are detrimental. The recognition can only come from within a person. They must have the ability to perceive. This is the reason why many people still smoke cigarettes and use harmful drugs despite the vast amounts of research proving the negative health effects. Until they can recognize the harmful effects in their own life by doing these actions, they will keep doing them. One of the biggest issues facing businesses and industries is knowledge transfer. Millions of dollars have been spent trying to find a solution to transfer knowledge from one person to another, without any success.

Recognition of the truth cannot be given to someone; it is a capability within themselves. It must be practiced and developed. In fact, it is one of the most important things to learn how to do and develop. This is something that is misunderstood in society. When a child is growing up, parents want them to be successful. They enroll them in multiple programs, such as sports, language training, and academic studies. Very rarely does a parent create an opportunity for a child to learn how to observe better. The ability to observe will help a child more than any other talent or skill. When a person learns how to observe, they learn how to recognize inaccuracies in their own perception of life. This person develops the intrinsic motivation and understanding to change themselves. This person will have the capability to go into any industry and occupation and improve at a rate faster than anyone else. By learning observation skills first, a child will also quickly realize what talents come naturally to them. Thus, by being able to learn quickly in an occupation that comes naturally to them, no one will be better than them. The one who can learn the quickest is the one who will become the greatest.

Many people think that the only reason people don't know something is because they have not been taught or do not have access to the right information. They think access to the information is the limitation, so they try to shove a lot of information and education at the child. However, they never realize that it is not the access to the information that prevented the child from learning; it was their inability to understand the information.

For example, if someone loses their hearing, no matter how much you talk to them, they will never be able to hear what you are saying. Same with talking in a different language. If the person doesn't understand your language, they will never understand what you are saying. You could try to talk with them for hundreds of days and it will be difficult to teach them. However, if you spend some time to teach them your language, they will learn much faster. If you give a deaf person a hearing aid or use sign language, they might learn from you a lot quicker. Teaching someone to observe is the trick to helping people learn and understand quickly. This has been proven many times.

In 1991, a music producer named, Gonzalo Garcia-Pelayo spent hours studying roulette tables and discovered that the results are not random. With the help of his family, Gonzalo started an initiative to document the results of roulette tables to create a prediction model. Gonzalo's model earned him $1.5 million over three years. Gonzalo soon started to observe other games of chance and would become the mentor of poker champion Carlos Mortensen. Gonzalo, like many other successful people, recognized one of the keys to understanding: observation (Garcia-Pelayo, 2017).

Observation is the most powerful of the five keys. Since truth identifies reality, and since reality is occurring at every moment, those who observe learn quicker and more accurately. When a person learns to observe, they can identify truth everywhere and in any circumstance. Thus, any truth must also be observable.

Albert Einstein understood this concept, as it always made him uncomfortable when a theory could not be observed in nature. His approach to science was from an observational approach. He stated, "I believe that, in order to make any real progress, one would again have to find a general principle wrested from Nature." (Albert Einstein – Biographical, 2014) Natural laws are always discovered, not created. This identifies that the ability to observe is critical to finding the truth. In fact, it is what drives innovation. Thus, a smart person is merely one who sees what is happening. It is through observation that Einstein was able to overcome the incorrect Newtonian notion of "absolute time" and discover the *Theory of Relativity* (Albert Einstein – Biographical, 2014). He simply identified that our perception of time changes depending on how fast we're moving. Hence, when an event occurs, it is relative to your motion and distance. Amazingly, to figure this out, you don't need to be a rocket scientist! However, this observation would be one of the main reasons for many advances in technology.

In science, they call this deductive reasoning or logic. It is where you observe a natural law and from there, make conclusions on reality. This is very different than the usual method of discovery, which is inductive reasoning. Many have found it difficult to differentiate between deductive and inductive reasoning. Induction requires the collection of facts, and from these facts patterns are identified to describe reality. Deduction looks at life from a very high level and induction looks at life from a very low level. One takes more observation and the other takes more critical thinking. Albert Einstein's view on this was as follows:

"The simplest picture one can form about the creation of an empirical science is along the lines of an inductive method.

Individual facts are selected and grouped together so that the laws that connect them become apparent...However, the big advances in scientific knowledge originated in this way only to a small degree...The truly great advances in our understanding of nature originated in a way almost diametrically opposed to induction. The intuitive grasp of the essentials of a large complex of facts leads the scientist to the postulation of a hypothetical basic law or laws. From these laws, he derives his conclusions" (Einstein, 1919).

People can become more observant by practicing elements of both inductive and deductive reasoning. As Einstein suggests, inductive methods tend to be more complex.

Four simple principles that will help you become more observant by focusing on big picture concepts are:

1. Moving slowly
2. Going with the flow
3. Thinking less
4. Being honest

Moving Slowly

During my college years, I had the opportunity to perform service with many older people in my church. Over a five-year span, I performed an average of fifteen hours of service a week. One of the many things that struck me during this time was the speed at which older people move; they are slow. The building that we worked in had very narrow hallways, and I would often get stuck behind one of them. At these times, I would think to myself, "Why do they move so slow?" Many of them had the capability to move faster, but rarely did. One day it finally dawned on me: as people get older, their body becomes more fragile. As people become more fragile, they must be more aware and observant of their environment since one accident could seriously injure them. Thus, they move slowly to become more aware of their environment to avoid injury. I realized that to increase my observational abilities, I too had to slow down. Older people have to do this due to age. I wondered how much better I could be if I learned to do this when I was young.

Moving slowly is not a skill or characteristic that is commonly associated with success. However, you will find that it is a characteristic of the most successful people. This is just as much a physical rule as it is a mental one. Intelligent people never rush into anything quickly. They take their time. They are in it for the long run. Here are some good examples:

1. Henry Ford – Was in his forties before he created a workable and sellable car (History.com Staff, 2009).
2. Momofuku Ando – Was 48 when he finally created a successful business selling Top Ramen and was sixty-one when he invented a cup of noodles (Hevesi, 2007).
3. Nelson Mandela – Was seventy-two years old before he was released from prison. Within the next ten years of his life he would receive more rewards than most people do in their life time, including the Nobel Peace Prize. In twenty years, Mandela would become loved and revered by the entire world (Keller, 2013).
4. Microsoft and Apple – Bill Gates and Steve Jobs are considered two of the most influential people to usher in the age of electronics and computers. This was no coincidence as both men, starting from their youth, spent all their time with computers and building products that would change the world. As Malcolm Gladwell pointed out, both had spent more than ten thousand hours working with computers and programming by the age of twenty-six (Gladwell, 2008).
5. Morgan Freeman – Was forty-four years old before he received a starring role in a movie (Biography.com, 2018).
6. Warren Buffett – Started investing when he was still in elementary school (Biography.com, 2018).

To move slowly, one must understand why people move fast. Simply put, people move fast because they think that what is in their head is more important than what is actually going on. Think about it. While in motion, someone will only avoid paying attention when they think they already know where everything is. Bigger people will look around less because they are less likely to get hurt by their environment. However, smaller people are more observant of their environment, because they are more likely to get stepped on or injured. When talking with someone, people will only stop to listen if they don't know what a person is going to say. In other words, those who think they know move faster than people who think they do not know. That is the mistake younger people make all the time. They think they know everything, so they don't listen. They don't listen in their classes, they don't listen to their parents, they don't listen to anyone. This is detrimental because the knowledge and understanding they would have gained is lost.

"Moving fast" is not exclusive to physical movement. Fast movers also possess the following characteristics:

1. They are always too busy.
2. They don't have time for anything, especially to learn to understand.
3. They are reactive. They don't have time to preplan or think things out, so they must take care of issues as they occur.
4. They don't accept ideas or thoughts from others. To do this, they would have to listen and see what others are saying. This would slow them down.
5. They physically move faster and perform actions that normally people consider "risky."

Due to advances in technology, life has become fast paced. The Millennial generation has been raised in a hyperactive society. One in which the senses are constantly being overloaded in every form possible. Multi-tasking has become the norm. It is even expected that, despite having to perform or be in a situation where your full and constant attention is needed, you should be able to do something else at the same time. In university classes, one of the major impediments to students learning is due to trying to listen, text, and look at social media at the same time. This basic idea is causing record breaking car accidents, as people try to use their cellphones and drive at the same time (Beauchamp, 2017). Especially among younger generations, people these days refuse to take a split second of downtime.

While this culture has helped some people feel like they get more done, it has created a big issue. With all this *doing*, no one is *observing* or accomplishing anything impactful. T.S. Elliot wrote, "Where is the life, we have lost in living? Where is the wisdom we have lost in knowledge? Where is the knowledge we have lost in information?" (Eliot, 1934) Society mistakenly believes that the ability to do things fast and take in information is the same thing as being productive. The opposite is true: the more someone tries to multi-task, the less they will accomplish (Merrill, 2012). Business has prevented us from being able to observe our surroundings. It has hampered our ability to understand reality and find the truth. It is no wonder that depression and suicide rates have been increasing (CDC, 2018).

Imagine driving a car in the city. When you first get going, you can see a clear picture of what is around and in front of you. You can even look at your rearview mirror to see behind you. It is easy to think of where you would like to go and how to find your way there. This is because you are going slow enough to give you time to observe and process. As your speed picks up to sixty mph, then to seventy mph, a couple of things happen:

1. Your focus shifts to only what is in front of you because it becomes difficult just to avoid hitting something.
2. You barely have time to look alongside your car; the outside becomes more of a blur.
3. You only look for objects that might cause a car accident instead of looking at the scenery.

Then your speed goes to eighty, ninety, one hundred mph. All your concentration now must be on making sure you don't crash. You have no time to think about your direction, about what is around you, or what is behind you. At certain speeds, it even becomes impossible to steer the car, and it ends by crashing into something.

This analogy is much like life. Those who go slower can direct their life in the way they would like. They can observe what is happening and make wise choices. They can appreciate the world, because they are not having to focus on avoiding obstacles. They have a clear and accurate picture of their surroundings and who people are. This enables them to be more efficient.

There are many ways in which society has tried to speed up life. As mentioned, one of these ways is by multitasking. Another disturbing trend I have seen in society has been trying to introduce children to mature concepts at a younger age. I have seen this with one of my nephews. His parents exposed him to a lot of information, hoping he would learn to read, write, and perform arithmetic sooner. The amazing thing is that it worked. He learned quickly, so he is a very smart boy. But the caveat is this: his mind was not given the time to develop fully. His technical ability has come at a price: he is unstable and immature. Compared to his brothers who were given more freedom to learn as they desired, he requires more supervision and guidance. In our advanced high school classes, we are finding the same issues. Many of these students have incredible technical capability, however, they are unstable. Stress and worry prevent them from feeling like they are in control. To them, slowing down is like trying to stop a car moving at two hundred mph. It can't be done very easily without incurring permanent damage.

It takes discipline to move slow, because when you move slow, you don't see immediate results. At first, it seems like the people moving fast are way ahead of you, but life is a long road. It is very much like the tortoise and the hare; sometimes you might not realize you are ahead until you reach the end of the race. It is better to develop correct principles and the ability to live a life consistently, than to be able to move fast. In fact, many times parents forget this idea the most. Due to their desire to make their kids successful, they have high expectations on how their kids use their time, requiring them to always be busy. They forget when they were young, how much time they had to waste, enjoy themselves, and figure life out. Now we want kids to figure their life out when they are still in elementary school. Society has seen the impact of this, students know more than ever in the history of mankind, but they are also the most unstable and unhappy (APA, 2017).

Going with the Flow
(The Law of Harmony)

The power of observation has been used by experts in all fields to discover groundbreaking advances. This is the concept that Bruce Lee used to become one of the greatest martial artists of all time. He realized that the ability to watch your opponent and move with their force instead of opposing them was the quickest and most efficient way to overcome them.

Bruce Lee's fighting style and beliefs were based on the idea of Naturalism. Naturalism being derived from the Chinese phrase "Wu-Wei," which is defined as Non-Action (Wu meaning "no" and Wei meaning "action") (Popova, 2018). The theory is that top performance is reached when the mind is free to react naturally. It is like a pitcher catching a ball hit directly at him. The ball is approaching too fast for the pitcher to consciously tell his mind to lift his hand and catch the ball. At that moment, he releases control of his mind and allows it to react on its own. When control is released, it quickens the pitcher's reaction and increases his accuracy in catching the ball. Lee's theory was that in fighting and in life, one must train the body and the mind to not resist the natural flow of life. One must be in complete harmony with it. Lee best explained this through the laws of non-interference and the law of harmony.

Lee describes the law of non-interference with nature as "... a basic principle of Taoism, that one should be in harmony with, not rebellion against, the fundamental laws of the universe. Preserve yourself by following the natural bend of things and don't interfere. Remember, never to assert yourself against nature; never be in frontal opposition to any problems, but to control it by swinging with it," (Lee, 2015).

He goes on to describe the law of harmony as, "The law of harmony, in which one should be in harmony with, and not in opposition to, the strength and force of the opposition. This means that one should do nothing that is not natural or spontaneous; the important thing is not to strain in any way."

Bruce Lee teaches that it is futile to try to resist another individual's natural actions. Instead, one must flow with that action. This is just as true in the realm of martial arts as it is in business or education. To try to change an individual's natural behavior takes a great amount of energy and resources; it is very inefficient. To maximize an individual's capability, it is important to align a person in a position where that person's natural behaviors can produce the desired results.

Bruce Lee teaches that the wise master will always mold his ways to fit the ignorant, and the ignorant will try to control everything to fit his/her own style. As Bruce Lee directs when facing opposition, "Cooperate with your opponent. Do not resist or interrupt his flow of movement. Instead of stopping his force, complete it by following him. In other words, you help him to destroy himself. Remember this - what you will do depends on your opponent; that is why we say — be the complement and not the opposite of the opponent's force." (To focus on the opponent means that it does not matter what is in your mind, but more what is in the mind of your opponent. In fighting, this means observing your opponent is more important than what you think).

Bruce Lee went to great lengths to help his students learn to observe their opponents, so they could go with the flow of the natural movement of the fight, instead of opposing it.

In life, to learn to observe reality, we must learn not to oppose it. Those who oppose reality might say:

1. "Life is unfair."
2. "That is a mistake," or "That never should have happened."
3. "You need to change. The way you are is not right."

All these statements are challenging or opposing what has happened or who people are. They promote not accepting what actually is, in favor of what you "think" it should be. In the next section you will find that "thinking" is one of the major acts that causes people to oppose reality.

Thinking Less

Scott Flansburg, also known as the "The Human Calculator," is known for his ability to perform complex math calculations in his head. Several tests have shown that his mind is quicker than a calculator. However, one of the most interesting discoveries regarding his ability is that when Scott is calculating math in his head, the activity in his brain is shown to be less than the activity in a regular person's brain. It has been a common idea that smart people think more; that their brain tends to be more active. However, scientific discoveries are now proving that the more intelligent you are the less you think (Flansburg, 2012). Scott explains that when he does calculations, he just sees the answer; he doesn't need to think about it.

Here is the logic of thinking less: when you see something that is simple, you do not have to think about it. The more complex it is, the more it requires you to think. You think when you don't understand. You don't understand because you lack information. For example, imagine that I am holding a water bottle a few feet above the ground. If I let go, what direction will the water bottle move? Without having to think or without having to see this in action, you instantly know that the water bottle would fall if I released it. When something is as simple as the law of gravity, there is no need to think about what happens when objects are dropped. The answers come naturally.

Contrary to popular opinion, thinking does not help you learn additional information. When you think, your mind must make up new information from what it knows. Thinking happens when the brain needs to draw a conclusion based on limited facts. If all the facts were present, the answer would be obvious, and there would be no need to think. Thus, the more you think, the more information you make up, and the more you make up, the better chance you will have inaccurate information. This problem is exacerbated when you realize that no one perceives everything 100 percent accurately. Thus, when you think, you are using inaccurate information to try to generate additional information. This brings a great amount of risk to being correct and to a person's life. Those who are more intelligent realize that thinking might not be the most efficient way to learn.

Figure 5 depicts how most people learn something new (the cycle of learning). They observe new information, then they think about the new information (so they can make a decision). When they feel they have thought about it enough, they apply it to their life, and successful application means a person has changed. Changing always leads to observing new information. A closer look (Figure 5) at the cycle reveals that one of the steps does not provide any value to learning new information. "Thinking" does not help a person observe more. Once a person sees new information, thinking about it doesn't change what it is. Until they apply it, they will never be able to get more information. Thus, the less time someone thinks about something and the quicker they act on it, the quicker they learn. This is why intelligent people tend to learn quick—because they spend less time thinking and more time doing.

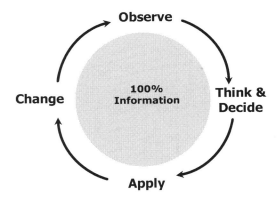

Figure 5: Learning Cycle (D. Kashiwagi, 2018)

Figure 6 shows the learning cycle of more intelligent people. They realize that thinking focuses more on what is in your mind rather than what is actually there. Thus, thinking hinders a person from seeing reality.

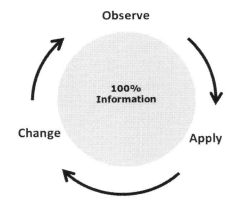

Figure 6: Advanced Cycle of Learning (D. Kashiwagi, 2018)

The opposite of thinking is observation. Figure 7 shows the different characteristics of No-Thinking (Figure 6) vs. Thinking (Figure 5).

Observation	**Thinking**
– Deductive	– Inductive
– Utilize knowledge of others	– Rely on own knowledge more
– Assume you do not know	– Assume your perception is correct
– Change more	– Change less
– More efficient	– Less efficient
– Less decision making	– More decision making
– Accepting of others	

Figure 7: Two Approaches to Thinking

Some of the characteristics of a person that observes are as follows:

1. Think less and observe more.
2. They apply/do more.
3. They listen.
4. They accept people and events for what they are.
5. They do not make judgements unless they know.
6. They do not make time for questionable things or people.
7. They figure out why instead of question why.

The idea of thinking less is not a popular idea with most academic leaders or parents. Telling students or children to sit and think about what they have done or what they have heard is a very accepted practice believed to be good for the student or child. However, when you identify what actually happens when students sit and think, it looks more like the child is being abused than helped. If a child or student did something wrong, by observation, they lack information. The only way to improve the act is by the child gaining new information. Sitting and thinking isolates the child from reality. It shuts them off from being able to gain any information, leaving them in a position that increases stress, worry, and confusion.

The idea that thinking is a good thing has been so engrained in society that people often do not realize the detriment of it.

A common question I ask when I visit high school students is, "If someone asks you to jump off a one-hundred-foot bridge with cement at the bottom, and you are not thinking, what would you do?"

The common answer is, "I would jump," but it is not the correct one. The reason people say this is because they associate the poorer choice with not thinking. However, explaining the correct answer to the students usually helps them realize their error. The logic is that if you were to jump off a one-hundred-foot bridge, you would die. You don't have to think about it; you know that. Hence, if you weren't thinking about it, you would not jump. It is what we call a no-brainer.

Now there are some people who don't know they would die, so they would "think" about if it is a good idea to jump. In fact, the people who think about it will most likely jump, because they will put aside the idea that they will die, and the following will go through their mind:

1. Who asked me to do it? Should I trust them?
2. Maybe something could happen, but I will be okay.
3. Why would they ask me to jump in the first place?

All these questions that people would think about are a lot more confusing than sticking to what they know, which is they will die if they jump. Those who don't think only stick with the information they know. Thus, if someone asks them to do something that requires thinking, they don't listen to the person.

The more we train our mind not to think, the more we focus on observing reality. I always ask students what is more important: what you think or reality? Of course, reality is more important. Those who cannot see what is happening have significantly more risk than those who can see. When looking at people who can't physically see, they have a lot more risk than those who can physically see. This is the same as understanding those who are mentally blind (those who do not listen and focus more on what they think than what is reality). They have a lot more risk than those who are willing to learn what is accurate and real.

Honesty

Honesty is a characteristic that can simplify life, minimize thinking in society, and increase success. This is a principle that parents usually try to instill in their children. However, if you were to ask many people why you should be honest, most could not tell you a logical reason. Some usual responses would be, "It is the right thing to do" and "It is the moral thing to do." But the question is, "*Why* should I do the right thing or the moral thing?"

Many people realize that being honest will make you more successful and bring a happier, less stressful life. But how? First, we need to identify what honesty is. When we say someone is honest, it means that they are identifying reality accurately, which means dishonesty is having a false perception of reality. Thus, the more dishonest you are, the more incorrect your perception is. Being able to observe reality accurately is a skill. The more you do it, the more accurate you become; the less you do it, the less accurately you can identify it. In other words, dishonesty brings inconsistency, inaccuracy, and an inability to observe. It requires a person to do more work and be less efficient, and in the long term it can hinder a person's ability to be successful. When a person is dishonest, they create another decision in their mind: to either accept or reject reality. The more someone rejects reality, the less capable they are of seeing it, and this impacts a person's ability to know what is happening.

Key #3: Summary

Observation is one of the most powerful keys to observing the truth. It takes more than just opening your eyes. It requires a person to minimize their thinking. People who observe do the following:

1. They move slowly, realizing no amount of activity can help them more than seeing reality.
2. They don't make decisions. If they don't know, they find someone who does.
3. They minimize their resistance to people, events, and ideas. When they don't agree with something, they try to collect more information. Instead of resisting reality, they adjust their mind to be in alignment with it.
4. They practice being honest all the time.

Observation is a tool that must be developed over time. As someone becomes more observant, they will be able to see reality more, and it will help them find truth.

Key #4:
Utilizing Expertise

While I was in grade school, I enjoyed playing American football with my friends. It was a physical sport. My parents would tell me not to play the game. They said I would get hurt, but since there were no rules in my house, I played anyways. It only took a couple of games until I was hit hard by a friend who weighed one hundred seventy pounds, and I broke both bones in my right forearm. Unfortunately, when I was injured, my parents were at a conference they were hosting. I waited for what seemed like forever for someone to take me to the hospital; the pain was tremendous. However, an interesting thing happened when I was in pain: I saw things clearly. When the body is in survival mode, the mind cannot afford to entertain false ideas; it is trying to find a solution to ensure that it never happens again. At this point I realized, I had no one to blame. I had to admit that I had been blind (another word for "not observant"). Using my newfound intelligence, the facts seemed to line up. I weighed ninety-nine pounds, I was five feet tall, and the people I was playing with were on the high school football team, most of them weighing more than one hundred and fifty pounds. Anyone with a bit of common sense could have predicted what would happen. Then it occurred to me why my parents had encouraged me not to play the game.

From the previous experience, you can probably guess I was not the smartest kid. Some of my characteristics include:

1. I was one of the few siblings who did not make it into any accelerated learning programs in elementary school or advanced placement classes in high school.
2. I had to attend speech therapy for most of my childhood.
3. I had a difficult time with school.
4. My mind did not naturally think logically.
5. I was a social outcast. I did not know how to interact with people. My friends were social outcasts.
6. I was fearful. When I was young, I was scared of the characters at amusement parks (like Snow White).
7. I was prideful, even though I had nothing to be proud of (that's a sign of someone who really doesn't understand).

Who I was enabled me to learn the greatest lesson in life: it is better to know how to utilize expertise than to be the expert. I had no other option. I realized that I had neither the intelligence nor the natural talent to be successful on my own. It took me much longer to understand that no one does. I found this to be one of the keys to finding truth as well. In observing my family, I recognized that no one is perfect, and I observed the following:

1. My parents would spank my older siblings (I felt this was not right; I saw pain and I didn't like it).
2. My father would tell me to do things, such as be patient, but then I would see times where he would not be patient.
3. I watched my brothers almost burn down our house with gasoline.
4. I saw my oldest brother get caught by the police for shoplifting.
5. My second oldest brother was a genius, smartest person I ever knew, but he didn't finish college.
6. I saw my sisters take off with their friends, without considering who would clean the house or take care of our younger siblings.

7. I even saw my own imperfections, such as losing my temper, arguing with my siblings and parents, and playing computer games for hours.

I perceived that my entire family was imperfect. I saw "bad" characteristics in each of them (especially in my siblings). This created a feeling that they were wrong, not worth listening to, and could not help me. This was accompanied by a feeling that I was "right."

However, with time and more observation, I started to recognize that everyone had their expertise, and they each helped me in their own way:

1. My genius brother would assist me in writing essays in grade school (he would write most of them). They were so good that two of the essays won awards, which brought me high praises. He was one of the reasons that I would get through my undergraduate industrial engineering degree in less than three years.

2. My sisters would assist me in asking girls out and dating ideas and activities. They were the reason I could convince an amazing girl to marry me.

3. My mother prevented me from getting married to a girl that wasn't right for me.

4. My younger brothers were well connected and could gather their friends to assist in activities and sporting events. They also helped me learn the value of people and being social.

5. My oldest brother was an expert at anything dealing with the outdoors and anything that explodes. He saved our entire scout unit on a hiking trip by building a huge bonfire before a storm hit our camp in freezing temperatures. He helped me get through my scouting program.

I learned the imperfection did not lie in the family, it was in me. The "right path" in life is whatever actually happens. My bias created an artificial "wrong path." I could not accept reality. Each of my siblings' "good" and "bad" characteristics allowed them to become experts in their own areas. When you realize everyone has their own unique expertise due to their unique characteristics and actions, then you can accept people for who they are and accurately identify their expertise.

You find the truth quicker and understand reality more, as you are able to utilize the expertise of everyone. Everyone knows something, and the more you listen to all people, the quicker you will find the truth and learn.

My interaction with my siblings enabled me to overlook the weaknesses of my father and realize that he knew more than anyone else. He was an expert in life. Thus, I realized that despite my weaknesses, if I listened to him, I would achieve and learn more than if I tried to go through life by myself. It is just common sense.

Engagement to "Stacy"

I met a girl at a dance competition in Arizona when I was twenty-three (we'll call her Stacy). Stacy was from Utah. To make a long story short, two months after meeting her, I was engaged to her. I made the decision that she was a good match for me.

My parents did not approve of Stacy. My mom was so distraught over the marriage, that I delayed the wedding date by six months. However, I was determined to make it work. I knew that my parents would be in Utah for a business trip, so I arranged for my parents to meet her parents. After this event, it seemed that my parents disapproved of the marriage even more. I obviously did not realize why they were telling me not to marry Stacy, but my intuition told me that I was missing something.

I remember one morning asking my father what he thought. He asked me, "Do you know what I look like when I am excited about something... do I look like I am excited?" Of course, his face looked like all the other times he saw any of his children doing something that he believed would cause us pain. I was a little blind, but I was smart enough to realize he wasn't happy.

I knew my time was running short; our marriage was in four weeks. I sat down with Stacy and asked her what she thought of our relationship and if we were ready. At the end of that conversation, I could tell that she had doubts as well. So, I asked her to lay-out a plan. The plan was as follows:

1. She would go to Utah and stay with her family.
2. We would not communicate for three weeks.
3. She would talk with her father, mother, family, and religious leaders.
4. She would spend time everyday writing down her thoughts regarding the marriage. What she felt. What she wanted. What she expected it to be.
5. She would write in her journal every day.

We carried out the plan. It took only one week before she called to ask to cancel the wedding. She had talked with her family and religious leaders. They told her that anyone who would not talk with his fiancé three weeks before their marriage did not love her.

After the marriage was cancelled, I was shaken. Seeing how close I was to marrying the "wrong" person was more of an eye opener than breaking my arm. I remember the arguments I had with my parents over the issue. I remember how I was 100 percent sure that I was right. Then I looked at the dominant information regarding Stacy and me:

1. Her family was struggling financially. They felt I would be the one to support them.
2. She was from a different social class mentality. She worked because she had to. I worked because I loved it.
3. For the month-and-a-half she was in Arizona, she did not fit in with any of my friends and family.
4. She did not enjoy any activities that I enjoyed.

5. There was a lot of talking. We had conversations regarding our relationship every night. It was tiring and consumed all my time.

After looking at the dominant information, it seems unbelievable that I could even have thought Stacy was a good match for me. Stacy was a great person; the issue was that we just didn't fit together. It is another experience that enforced the idea of listening to the expert. I realized that the expertise of both of my parents saved me.

Overcoming Bias and Listening Experts

You do the most reflection after something goes wrong. One idea that came to mind while reflecting on my cancelled wedding to Stacy was why I had so many arguments with my father. I realized it was because I still thought I knew when I didn't. I still gave myself too much credit. So, I looked at the dominant information regarding my father:

1. He was 30 years older than me. That was more than twice my age!
2. He was world renowned for his construction management process.
3. His efforts led to changing the supply chain in an entire country (Netherlands).
4. I have seen him solve hundreds of people's problems for more than twenty years. I remember seeing him talk with our sixty-year-old neighbors. They had been married for a long time. After all those years of being married, it wasn't until my father talked with them that the wife realized what the husband was thinking.
5. I have never seen his efforts go to waste at anything (100% success rate).
6. He has a Ph.D., he is a full professor, and he was a professional engineer.

7. He had built a non-traditional multi-million-dollar research group.

8. He had eight children and had been married for more than thirty years.

9. He had provided financial support for every sibling in one way or another.

From that point on, I have tried to minimize arguments with my father. It is not logical to be telling him what to do or what is right. I was thirty years younger and had an undergraduate degree. I realized I needed to listen more and learn. Who in their right mind would try to tell someone with the performance metrics of my dad what to do? Only a "blind" child would.

Throughout my life, I have defended my father and supported his ideas. I have tried to spend as much time with him as I could. The family feels it is because I am the closest to my dad and most like him, so I have a bias. My co-workers felt it was due to him being my father. However, they were all wrong. It was because I realized he was an expert. I realize that by staying close to him, he would teach me to be an expert as well. I often would wonder why others did not see this.

Thus, while other family members might have felt that our father was very controlling, I was trying to figure out what he knew and understand why he was asking me to do certain things. It wasn't about the rules, it was about becoming a better person. I realized he wasn't trying to control us, but to teach us what he knew.

A person who does not have as much expertise will never understand the actions of an expert. Just as a child will never understand the parent. They will always feel like the expert/parent is making a mistake. However, those who understand logic will always try to listen and learn, instead of trying to use the imperfections of the expert/parent (which they will definitely have) to justify going against them. The understanding person realizes that if they listen, the following will happen:

1. They will learn. They will be able to understand the difference between what they thought and what the expert thought. The expert will explain the difference in a dominant and logical way.
2. The expert will make mistakes, but there will be less mistakes made by listening than by not listening.
3. When mistakes happen, they will learn from them and gain more expertise. They will utilize many more years of experience and expertise.

Utilizing Expertise

In 2009, Simon Sinek published a book called *Start with Why?* He identified that successful leaders' organizations used the "why" to sell their cause and product instead of the "what" and "how" (Sinek, 2011).

Children from a young age seem to ask one question most often: "Why?" Due to their lack of information and the complexity of the world, they desire to figure out what is going on. Children inherently accept that they don't know a lot about the world, so they are willing to ask "Why?" Many people struggle because they think they know something when they really don't, so they never ask, "Why?"

One of the quickest ways to identify if a belief or an opinion is accurate and matches with reality is to go through a two-phase process. The first phase is asking yourself a simple question: How do you know? The second phase is then explaining to yourself how you know. The first phase is the hardest to remember; the second phase takes the intelligence.

A study was performed testing people's ability to make decisions. The study found that when making decisions, the people who felt they were experts performed worse than freshman college students, and a computer algorithm performed better than everyone (Snijders et. al., 2003). Research shows that human beings are not good at making logical conclusions. Often, they make decisions based on feelings instead of facts. They make decisions based on what they don't know, rather than what they do know. They aren't willing to ask "Why?"

Research has identified that human beings are not good decision makers. Multiple psychologists have performed studies finding the following about people:

1. They do not see the world as it is, but as it is useful to see (Beau Lotto, PhD).
2. The brain can only focus on one thing at a time. Thus, people miss many things due to unintentional blindness (Daniel Simons, PhD).
3. People do not have good memories and will believe and remember things that didn't happen (Elizabeth Loftus, PhD).
4. Most decisions come due to emotions instead of using logic and information (Antonio Damasio, PhD).
5. They tend to believe their own thought even when facing overwhelming opposing evidence (cognitive dissonance).
6. People cannot accurately identify their own capability.

The human brain causes risk. The question is, how do you minimize the risk caused by the human brain? We first must identify when we rely on the brain the most. As mentioned in the "Thinking Less" section of Key 3, we tend to rely on the brain when we have to think more. Returning to the water bottle example, you know what's going to happen when I drop an object because it is simple. As things get complex, more thinking is needed. How do we create a world that is not complex? With so many variables in the world, it is very difficult to find out the relationships and how one thing impacts another. In the next chapter, we will identify a way to make this easier.

People usually think the only way to understand life is to memorize and develop a mind that is powerful. However, that is impossible and can never happen. In my class at Arizona State University, I show students the diagram below (Figure 8). When you look at life on an information scale (with zero equaling not knowing anything, and one hundred equaling knowing how the flaps of butterfly wings in Africa impact the atmosphere in the U.S.), how much information does any individual actually know? The answer is almost zero.

With all the information that we do not know, when you look at life like this, it seems foolish to take the little information we have gained through our experience and understanding and expect it to help us with everything we don't know. There is a better way that brings less risk. I teach my students it is the way they can know everything without knowing anything. All you must do is utilize the expertise of others and technology; they enable you to have 100 percent information without knowing anything (see the Figure 8).

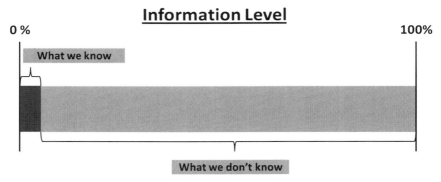

Figure 8: Information Level Chart

The older a person becomes, the more they understand this concept. If you watch the elderly, you find that they do this better than anyone. When they need to setup an email account, they are not going to learn the technology; they will find someone young to help them. In no time at all they will have an email account setup, and before you know it, the child will be writing their emails for them as well. Knowing how to utilize expertise helps you to increase your efficiency and improve the quality of work and service you receive. Those who have this skill have more time to spend on activities they enjoy, and they can relax more.

Sometimes students say, "Well, if everyone does this, then there will be no one to do the work." That is only true if everyone utilizes expertise, but everyone doesn't do this. In fact, most people don't have the capability to do it, and many people don't want to do it even if they could. There are thousands of engineers graduating from college every day, but how many of those engineers know how to utilize the other engineers to produce something of value to society? The answer is almost none. In other words, it is better to be able to utilize expertise than to be the one who knows.

Key #4: Summary

This key is the easiest to implement. It requires no capability to perform. However, it does require humility. The action is simple: when you don't know, you ask someone who does know. People who use this key do the following:

1. They listen.
2. They don't focus on people's imperfections, they focus on people's talents and strengths.
3. When they don't know something, they tell people that they don't know.
4. They search for people who are experts at things they need.

Key #5:
Taking the Extreme

The ability to differentiate is important in life. This skill determines much of a person's ability to control their life and to get what they want. The logic is simple. If everything was the same, then it wouldn't matter who you are, what you choose, or what you have. That's because the outcome, the enjoyment, the difficulty, and the result will always be the same. However, in life, that is not the case. In fact, everything is very different.

Thus, when you can tell the difference between paths in life, people, or things, it enables you to more accurately identify outcomes and events. The younger a person can start to realize the differences between things, the more intelligent and successful they will be.

I see examples of this each week when I go to church. I sit down and observe families with children around me. Some children are very noisy. When they talk, their voices are loud. When they move, they bang into things and move all over the place. Other children are quiet. When they speak, it is in a whisper. When they move, it is slowly. The main reason for the difference is that one child can differentiate between a playground and a church, and the other child cannot. The noisy child doesn't realize that in one place everyone is quiet, dressed nicely, and is sitting down, while in the other environment people are dressed to play and the noise level is high.

As children get older, it is easier for them to differentiate, although some have a really difficult time even after they get older.

Not being able to differentiate is the reason most people have an issue with life, or, in other words, think that life is unfair. This also leads to stress, worry, and depression. For example, take an event with two siblings (see Figure 9). Sibling 2 feels like the family mistreats them. You can definitely understand why when you look at the different outcomes of each sibling. Sibling 2 thinks that they both have identical initial conditions since they were raised in the same family. However, the final conditions are not the same. In other words, they can't tell any difference, but they see they get different outcomes. This leads to the belief that life is unfair.

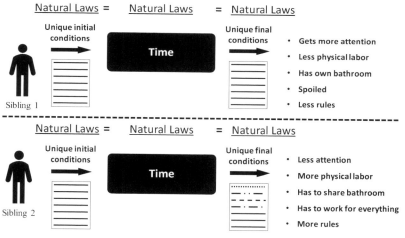

Figure 9: Event Charts for two siblings.

From the parents' perspective, it is not unfair. In fact, they believe it is the only way to operate and treat both children. They can clearly see how the initial conditions are different. Figure 10 shows a difference Sibling 2 overlooked: one is a boy and the other a girl. When children are young, they don't understand the difference between gender. The boy doesn't understand that, on average, young girls typically need more personal space. Most young girls tend to be more conservative and less violent, thus they need less rules.

Sibling 1   Sibling 2

Figure 10: Gender is a unique condition.

This happens all the time in life. At one point, I was taking dance lessons with my sister. We happened to stay after our lessons one day to overhear an instructor complaining about some other students. He went on about how people do not realize how difficult it is to become a professional dancer. He said he spends hours each day teaching people to dance, practicing himself, and has spent years going through dance training and competitively dancing. Then he identified how students expect to dance for a couple of hours a week and then become just as good as he is at dancing. This is not even considering his genetic and natural ability to dance. Oftentimes in life we do the same thing. We look at others and have no idea what they have been through or who they are, but we think that we are the same and that we should get the same result as them.

This is really the reason and purpose for science and experiments—to find the difference. Being able to tell the difference helps you to see the truth or understand reality.

There have been multiple experiments conducted to show the impact of characteristics of children that lead to success, the little things children do that we overlook but that have a great impact on their future. One such experiment divided kids by their ability to wait one minute to eat a marshmallow (Mischel, 1989; Urist, 2014). The kids were sat down and were told that if they waited until the adult came back to eat the marshmallow, they would get another marshmallow. They found out the majority couldn't wait. However, the most interesting thing about this study is that they followed these children into adulthood, and they found a difference. The kids who waited to eat the marshmallows were found to have a greater amount of success in life than those who didn't. Being able to tell the difference helps to predict the future and find the truth. To see cause and effect, a person first must be able to differentiate the initial conditions.

One way to look at this is with different types of food. Someone's dietary needs are dependent on their lifestyle. If you are exercising and wanting to build muscle, you eat foods with more protein in them. If you are exercising and performing a lot of cardio exercises, then you will need more sugar and carbohydrates. If you are sick and in need of nutrients, you will be eating more liquids and vegetables. It is important to learn the difference between foods, so you can get the optimal results. If you don't know the difference and you try to build muscle by eating lots of sugar, it won't work, it will get frustrating, it will cause more pain, and more than likely you will be disappointed. There are different optimal diets for different situations. People are like the different foods. The more you understand the difference, the more you realize every person has value. And if you do not know the difference, you will have a lot of expectations that will cause disappointment and pain.

This is the biggest impact of not being able to tell the difference between people—that you can't accurately identify the difference between yourself and others. This causes high expectations and a lot of disappointments. For example, it has caused an incorrect idea to be cultivated in society that identifies some jobs are more important than other jobs, and some people are more valuable than other people. Look at it this way: who is more important, a janitor or a rocket scientist? Most people would say the scientist. However, if we had no janitors, then buildings would not be maintained and cleaned. Eventually, the scientists would have to clean, and that would take them away from their inventions and testing. We find that both are important to an efficient life. The janitors perform a duty that is essential, just like the scientist, and both working together make an efficient system.

There was a documentary on Yellowstone National Park that a student introduced me to (*Wolves in Yellowstone National Park*, 2017). When settlers started moving westward, they killed off much of the wolf population to keep the area safe. They thought that killing the wolves would make for a better environment. The vibrancy and wildlife of the park was tracked for some years, and it turns out that without the wolves, the park did not do as well. Without the wolves, some animals dwindled, while others started to over-populate the park, which then led to a decrease in greenery and vibrancy of the park. Even the flow of rivers was altered because of the wolves' absence. Because people could not understand the necessity of all the animals and their differences, the park made an unwise decision to eliminate the wolves. Some years later, the park reintroduced the wolves and returned the ecosystem to its former glory.

Part of the difficulty in differentiating is due to the complexity in life or the multiple variables involved. To know all the variables is difficult, but then to also know how one variable affects the rest of the variables becomes an impossible task. It is like the puzzles in newspapers that ask you to identify the differences between two pictures. It is very difficult to identify the few minor changes since the pictures are so similar. It is the same in life. The child finds it difficult to differentiate between sitting at church and home, because of the similarities. In both places, they are with their family. In both places, they have their toys and coloring books. In both places, they are in a building. It doesn't occur to them that one place has other people around, one place has everyone sitting down, etc.

To differentiate, you must be able to do three things: observe the current situation, remember other situations, and be able to compare the two. Thus, people who can't differentiate have a problem with one or more of the steps (unable to observe, to remember, or to compare), with the third step being the most difficult. Earlier in this book, we identified that the mind cannot do any of these things well. It is no wonder most people have a difficult time getting what they want in life.

The mind needs help to be able to differentiate. Movie producers understand this. They realize that when someone is watching the film, they will not be able to see everything that the camera is filming. In fact, they realize there is too much information on the screen at any given time, and if the viewer is required to look at everything, they will get lost and have a difficult time following the story. The secret is in the focus of the camera. You will notice that, in movies, the camera will never put everything in focus. It will only focus on the main characters or event that is taking place, and everything in the background or around the scene that is not relevant will be out of focus. The camera also zooms in on the main characters. This creates a big contrast that enables the viewer to easily observe the information that is most important in the movie.

This is much like highlighting passages in a book or reading CliffsNotes. The highlighting distinguishes important pieces of information so that one can quickly go through an entire book by only looking at the relevant information. The focusing of the camera and the highlighting of passages enables a person to have a good idea of what is occurring without knowing everything. This is the same with life and people. It is impossible to know everything, and if you try, you will most likely get lost and confused. But focusing your attention on the right information will enable you to get a good picture without knowing everything.

Defining Extremes

One of the ways to focus the mind on the right information and minimize confusion is by taking extremes. The idea is simple: when two subjects are very different, you need less information to tell them apart. For example, if I were to hold up two brand new markers that were the same brand and color, it would be difficult to tell them apart if I mixed them up. You would need to study the markers and find a small scratch or imperfection to be able to differentiate the two. This would take a lot more information. However, if I were to hold up a marker that was black and one that was red of different brands, you could tell immediately the difference without further inspection.

Extremes simplify life, because they enable you to quickly differentiate between two things, whether it is people, objects, or the outcomes of two actions. It helps you to find the general rule without the need for a lot of information. For example, if you wanted to know if eating one piece of candy a day had a detrimental effect on your health, you would need to perform a lot of studies and carefully observe your body to figure out the impact of the one candy. However, if you take it to the extreme and ask if eating a bag of candy a day for ten years would have a detrimental effect on your health, it is much easier to conclude, and in many cases, you would not even need to eat the candy to figure it out.

My father, Dr. Dean Kashiwagi, developed a model called the Kashiwagi Solution Model (KSM). He used this model to help my siblings and me quickly differentiate people with minimal information. The model is simple and can be seen in Figure 11. The box is split into two sections. The Left Side (LS) identifies a person who perceives more information. The Right Side (RS) identifies a person who perceives less information. The two sides of the box are very similar to an Asian idea called the Yin and the Yang. In the KSM, you put any characteristics of people into the left and right sides of the box. For example, someone who perceives more information is more likely to be educated. So, education goes in the LS and no education goes in RS.

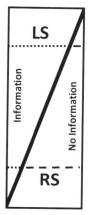

Figure 11: An example of a LS/RS KSM diagram. (D. Kashiwagi, 2018)

There are two major things to remember when using the KSM:

1. All LS and RS characteristics are relative and related.
2. Because no one has all information, everyone has a degree of LS and RS characteristics. We use the extreme only to tell the difference, but everyone is somewhere in the middle.

When I say the LS and RS characteristics are relative, what I mean is that determining how much of a characteristic you have is dependent upon who you are comparing yourself with. For example, if a ten-year-old is comparing themselves with a fifty-year-old, usually this comparison will make it seem like the ten-year-old is a lot more RS than the fifty-year-old. A better comparison would be the ten-year-old with others that same age. This might make the ten-year-old look a lot more LS than his peers. Since the model is relative, it is important to know the people you are comparing.

The KSM characteristics are also related. This means that once you find one characteristic that is exhibited strongly in a person, you will also find that person has all the other characteristics related to the RS or LS side. The relationship between all the RS and LS characteristics is what makes this such a powerful tool. It allows people to quickly know who someone else is with very little information.

The rest of this section will review some commonly mistaken characteristics and provide explanations for why they are on either the LS or RS of the KSM. Figure 12 below shows each of the traits discussed in this section and how they are all related to observing more information versus being unobservant to information.

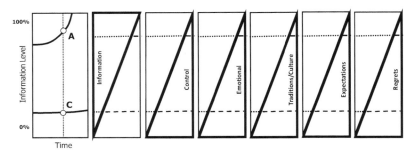

Figure 12: KSM diagram showing various key attributes. (D. Kashiwagi, 2018)

1. Accepting People vs. Trying to Control People

   The more information you have, the more you realize that no matter how much you try, everyone is unique and has different circumstances, and it is impossible to change a person. An example would be a parent trying to make their child play baseball when the child does not have good vision and hand eye coordination. No matter how much the child plays baseball, the parent can't make them become a great baseball player. The parent who understands their child better will accept who their child is and not try to make them do something that doesn't fit who they are.

2. No Emotion vs. Being Emotional

   Looking at the different emotions, one finds that people have them due to a lack of information. Take anger. The only reason a person becomes angry is when they thought they knew what would happen, but something else happens that they didn't expect, and they didn't like. Usually anger comes after being surprised. When a person knows in advance what will happen, they don't get as angry. The same is with excitement. When are you more excited? The first time you ride a roller coaster ride or the one hundredth time? As people gain more information, they become more stable and less emotional.

3. No Traditions/Culture vs. Having Traditions/Culture
    When you look at the definition of tradition and culture, it becomes apparent whether they are right or left side characteristics. A tradition is something you do the same way over a long period of time. The more culture you have, the more you act the same way over a long period of time. This means the more culture and tradition you have, the less you change. The less you change, the less information you perceive. This would mean that tradition and culture are on the right side. Many people do not like this idea, because they associate many enjoyable memories and feelings to traditions like celebrating Christmas or another religious holiday. Along with that could be unwrapping presents under the Christmas tree or cutting down a Christmas tree as a family. I always ask people, "What would you rather have, doing things the same way every year, or improving how you celebrate every year and making it better?" Those who want to improve and make it better are usually more LS.

4. No Expectations vs. Having Expectations
    Those who understand the natural laws realize that nothing happens by chance. Thus, people's actions are determined by who they are. More intelligent people realize they do not know everything. Thus, when they have the information and know what a person will do, they know it, and they do not need to expect anything. When they don't have the information and they don't know what will happen, they admit they do not know enough and they accept whatever actions a person performs.

Realizing that if a person ever acts in a different way than they thought they would, their mind is inaccurate, not the person's actions.

5. No Regret vs. Having Regrets
    Those with information realize that the event can only happen according to natural law, meaning nothing ever happens that is not required. Although, people might not be "perfect," their actions will always be in accordance with who they are and what everyone needs in their environment. Thus, the more people understand, the less they regret their actions. They also realize that although in the future they will change, it was required that they commit the action when they did so that they and those around them could learn and grow, realizing that life always follows natural law, and everyone experiences what they need.

Key #5: Summary

By taking the extreme, we can understand reality and identify truth quicker. Extremes allow us to easily compare two ideas without requiring a lot of data to differentiate between options. This helps identify accurate concepts. People who use this key do the following:

1. They ask themselves what is more likely. Instead of trying to collect 100 percent of the information before acting, they take the extreme and say which side is more likely to take me to the place I want to go, and then they move in that direction.
2. They look for differences in situations they don't understand, which helps them to understand cause and effect.
3. They gravitate toward ideas and people that make life simple and clear.
4. They match characteristics against observant and non-observant people, which can help determine the path to the greatest success.

APPLYING THE 5 KEYS:
No Influence Leadership

There are many truths, or natural laws, in life. Some might not have a clear impact in your life, but when they are discovered they totally change your world. There is one truth that is unknown to most, and when it's understood, it changes lives. If people understood this law that I speak of, it would change their motivation, their thinking, and their actions. It would affect every relationship they have and how they interact with people.

This truth is No Influence. This means one person cannot influence another person or be influenced by another person.

We will use all the keys we have been discussing in the previous chapters to discover the truth of this idea, except for *Key 3: Power of Observation*. That key cannot be shown in this chapter, because it must be something that you do on your own. You must take this information and begin to observe, watch, and begin to see the accuracy of the information in your own life.

What is Influence?

Before we get into the accuracy of the idea, first let's look at the impact of it in our lives. There are many definitions of influence. I have found the simplest explanation is when one person tries to control or change another person. Some different ways to explain influence:

1. The ability of an individual to change another individual.
2. When someone experiences a change caused by an external force without their consent.
3. When an individual through his or her actions causes another individual to:
   - Change the way he/she acts.
   - Change his/her attitude toward a certain action/task/concept/idea.
   - Desire something different than he/she had desired before.
   - Change the quickness of the person's growth/understanding/perception.

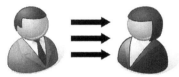

Figure 13: A Leader and a Follower

People often will change with the acquisition of more information and understanding. The question is, "Who determines what type of information is learned and how much information is transferred to an individual?" Influence denotes that a person's environment (i.e., everyone around the individual, such as family, friends, strangers, leaders, etc.) determines the amount of information that is transferred, understood, and acted upon. Figure 13 shows that in an organization, the leader is the one controlling the transfer of information to the follower. This is the same with a parent to a child or a teacher to a student. The general belief is that to some degree, the people around a person influence that person. That at some point in everyone's life, a mentor motivated you to go after your dream, a friend pressured you into doing an act that wasn't smart, or a teacher provided you with information or the opportunity that helped you to find success. The question is: how do we know they were influenced? How do we know that the motivation didn't come from within themselves, or that they deep down inside wanted to do the act, or that they would have discovered the information anyway?

We will use *Key #1: Knowing That You Don't Know*, to identify if the idea of influence is based off evidence or a biased opinion.

The first step is to identify if there is overwhelming information showing that the idea of influence has worked. I performed this research on influence for my master's thesis (Kashiwagi, 2007). I searched hundreds of articles and books to find if there was any study, research, or empirical evidence showing that the idea of influence is correct, and I found nothing. I found no information proving the idea that one person can truly influence another person. There are many leadership philosophies and programs based on the idea of influence, but none of them had any evidence that the idea of influence was correct (see Figure 14).

And it goes even further. When looking at the results of programs based on the idea of influencing people, I found that almost all those programs did not work in obtaining the results they were looking for. In fact, the programs that did not focus on influencing people always had higher results than the influence programs. This study entailed the following:

1. Looked at more than two hundred articles and books.
2. Surveyed one hundred seventy professionals on what ideas helped them more, the "influence" idea or "no-influence" idea.

After realizing there is no supporting evidence showing that a person can be influenced, I started to identify that the idea might not be right. This might be something that everyone thinks they know, but they don't.

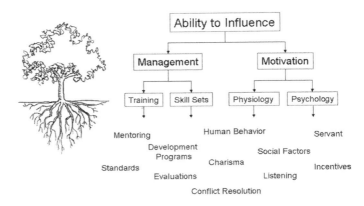

Figure 14: Many leadership concepts stem from the idea of influence

This led me to using *Key #4: Utilize Expertise*. The question was now, "What do successful people think?" This led me to do the following research: I investigated more than fifteen experts in multiple industries and various fields of study (martial arts, automobile manufacturing, commercial manufacturing, self-improvement, business, management, law, and politics). These experts lived at various times throughout history. The list included Niccolo Machiavelli, Socrates, Mozart, Mahtma Ghandi, Nelson Mandela, Edwards Deming, Jim Collins, Jack Welch, Bruce Lee, Soichiro Honda, Peter Drucker, James Allen, Abraham Lincoln, Rudolph Giuliani, Scott Flansberg, Ricardo Semler, Marcus Buckingham, Jack Ma, and Albert Einstein.

Although all these experts do not necessarily totally agree with the idea of no-influence, all their success came from ideas of no-influence. These experts came to believe in the principles of no-influence through the following:

1. Statistical Analysis (W. Edwards Deming).
2. Study of the most successful organizations within the last decade (Jim Collins).
3. Study of historical precedence and results of other countries (Niccolo Machiavelli).

4. Abnormal success and advances in a specific field of study (Bruce Lee, Jack Welch, Soichiro Honda, Mahatma Gandhi, Mozart, Nelson Mandela, Peter Drucker, and James Allen).
5. In-depth interviews of eighty thousand managers (Buckingham and Coffman).
6. Followers' approval ratings (Abraham Lincoln).
7. Philosophy and deductive reasoning (Socrates).
8. Physics (Einstein).

When utilizing the expertise of people who have proven themselves to be experts in the past, the idea of influence starts to lose credibility and increasingly looks like the idea could be inaccurate.

Let's look at what the idea of influence is really saying.

The idea itself is an exception. It is denoting that in some minor way the individual is being changed from his/her natural state by another person. In other words, an individual has control over themselves "except" when someone is influencing them.

The concept of "influence" does not follow the rules established by Key 2: No Exceptions. People tend to think that strong leaders are very influential, but the idea of influence contradicts many characteristics and philosophies that make someone successful. The next sections will compare the idea of no-influence to the following ideas commonly associated with successful people:

1. Accountability
2. Attraction
3. Liberty/Freedom

Influence vs. Accountability

The idea of influence has relieved most people in society to be accountable for their actions. If a person can be augmented by their environment, it allows individuals a multitude of variables on which to blame their failures. The idea of influence allows a person to believe they are not in complete control of their own life. However, if a person does not have complete control of their own life, how much control do they have? This is a question that cannot be answered, since there has been no proven method or formula to explain how to determine if a person does not have control. Therefore, a person can never be held accountable for anything, because you can never tell what they have control over and what they don't. The idea of influence also discredits those who truly perform, because there are a multitude of variables that people can claim helped them to succeed (social status, connections, resources, mentor, etc.). The idea of influence has reduced the importance of talent and skills in achievement and emphasized the importance of "luck."

James Allen teaches on the other side of the spectrum of influence, which is total accountability. His belief is that an individual is in complete control of their own life, meaning they not only determine their own environment, but also the circumstances in which they find themselves in. James Allen states, "In a justly ordered universe, where loss of equipoise would mean total destruction, individual responsibility must be absolute. A man's weakness and strength, purity and impurity, are his own, and not another man's; they are brought about by himself, and not by another; and they can only be altered by himself, never by another. His condition is also his own, and not another man's."

The debate between influence and accountability has been the cause of many arguments and lawsuits. In society it seems that influence is more widely accepted. It has become a foreign concept to say when a person succeeds it is due to his/her own hard work and effort, and when a person fails it is due to his/her own laziness and lack of preparation. The idea of influence is directly at odds with accountability.

In his book, *As a Man Thinketh,* James Allen (1900) proposes that it is impossible to prove that one person can influence or control another. He proposes that if a person is accountable, the universe is governed by logic, and if a person controls his/her own destiny, then influence cannot exist. Although it seems as if one person may influence or control another, it may be that the person being influenced chooses to be around the "influencer". In that case, the person is choosing who they listen to and learn from, so accountability falls on them. Allen proposes that a lack of information leads some to conclude that one person can influence or control another. Allen also reinforces that the principle of influence neither follows the laws of logic nor fits into the concept of accountability.

James Allen said, "As a being of power, intelligence, and love, and the lord of his own thoughts, man holds the key to every situation and contains within himself that transforming and regenerative agency by which he may make himself what he wills." James Allen explains that people control their own thoughts, and because of this they control who they become. "Man is a growth by law, and not a creation by artifice, and cause and effect are as absolute and undeviating in the hidden realm of thought as in the world of visible and material things. A noble and God-like character is not a thing of favor or chance but is the natural result of continued effort in right thinking, the effect of long-cherished association with God-like thoughts." James Allen pushed a concept that people are accountable for who they are, an idea that goes against the common belief. The logic that proves a person is accountable is as follows:

1. Everything is governed by law.
2. Individuals control their own thoughts.
3. Every thought by law will produce a certain outcome.
4. Hence, a person is accountable for their actions.

"As a man thinketh in his heart, so is he not only embraces the whole of a man's being but is so comprehensive as to reach out to every condition and circumstance of his life. A man is literally what he thinks, his character being the complete sum of all his thoughts." (Allen, 2012) James Allen believed that the thoughts of an individual not only developed his/her own character, but also was the cause of his/her environment and circumstances in life, "...man is the master of thought, the molder of character, and the maker and shaper of condition, environment, and destiny."

James Allen explains how thought controls circumstance. "Men imagine that thought can be kept secret, but it cannot; it rapidly crystallizes into habit, and habit solidifies into circumstance...."

Allen then goes on to identify the resulting circumstances of "evil" and "good" thoughts, "...Bestial thoughts crystallize into habits of drunkenness and sensuality, which solidify into circumstances of destitution and disease: impure thoughts of every kind crystallize into enervating confusing habits, which solidify into distracting and adverse circumstances; thoughts of fear, doubt, and indecision crystallize into weak, unmanly, and irresolute habits, which solidify into circumstances of failure, indigence, and slavish dependence......On the other hand, beautiful thoughts of all kinds crystallize into habits of grace and kindliness, which solidify into genial and sunny circumstances: pure thoughts crystallize into habits of temperance and self-control, which solidify into circumstances of repose and peace...."

Allen describes "The outer world of circumstances shapes itself to the inner world of thought, and both pleasant and unpleasant external conditions are factors which make for the ultimate good of the individual. As the reaper of his own harvest, man learns both of suffering and bliss." Man is truly accountable both for the "good" and the "bad" in his life, "...circumstances grow out of thought. Every man who has for any length of time practiced self-control and self-purification will have noticed that the alteration in his circumstances has been in exact ratio with his altered mental condition."

"When he begins to reflect upon his condition and searches diligently for the law upon which his being is established, he then becomes the wise master, directing his energies with intelligence and fashioning his thoughts to fruitful issues. Such is the conscious master, and man can only thus become by discovering within himself the laws of thought. This discovery is totally a matter of application, self-analysis and experience." James Allen teaches that change cannot happen from external forces (i.e., influence from others), but must come from within an individual. Hence, every individual has control over his/her own destiny. As Allen says, "The 'divinity that shapes our ends' is in ourselves; it is our very self."

James Allen reviews two common scenarios that have led people to believe in influence. However, he creates a different perspective that explains how the individual is really in control of and accountable for their lives.

The Abused and the Abuser

The scenarios of the tyrant oppressing the masses, the master enslaving his servants, and the criminal victimizing the helpless are always referred to in proving that it is possible to control others against their will (or influence in a negative way). However, this is only because we assume that no one wants to be abused, victimized, or controlled. With the discovery of more information into human psychology we find that, as absurd as it might seem to the average person, it is possible that the reason there is a need for tyrants, masters, and criminals is due to the desire of people to be controlled, oppressed, and victimized.

Allen says, "It has been usual for men to think and to say, 'Many men are slaves because one is an oppressor; let us hate the oppressor.'" Now, however, there is amongst an increasing few a tendency to reverse this judgment, and to say, "One man is an oppressor because many are slaves; let us despise the slaves." However, James Allen goes on to state, "The truth is that oppressor and slave are co-operators in ignorance and, while seeming to afflict each other, are afflicting themselves... He who has conquered weakness and has put away all selfish thoughts belongs neither to oppressor nor oppressed. He is free."

Persuasion

Persuasion, a form of influence, occurs when an individual declares one thing and then, through interacting with another person, changes their mind. This common occurrence in life, regularly observed, is one of the causes for the belief in "influence". James Allen explains that often people will say something that they might wish for, fancy, or want, but it does not match up with their innermost desires. He states, "Men do not attract that which they want, but that which they are... Not what he wishes and prays for does a man get, but what he justly earns. His wishes and prayers are only gratified and answered when they harmonize with his thoughts and actions." When a person seemingly changes his/her actions, position, mood, etc., after interacting with another person, the cause might not be due to the other person's influence, the situation might just be revealing the true desires of the individual. In many instances this is obvious, as when someone is only declining a gift out of politeness and then is coaxed into accepting it, or when someone nods in agreement to deflect an argument but later reveals that he/she did not truly agree with the person. However, when a person is very "convincing" or charismatic, it is easier to think the individual was influenced.

James Allen truly believed that "The soul attracts that which it secretly harbors...." It is only due to the complexity of life and multiple variables in an individual's environment that it seems a person is controlled by external variables. We end up finding that "Circumstance does not make the man; it reveals him to himself."

Influence vs. Attraction

The idea of influence is so engrained in society, that even the best experts have bought into the idea without thinking about its implications.

John Maxwell, founder of many leadership organizations such as Maximum Impact, is a well-known leadership expert. He has written more than thirty books, and his principles have been communicated to more than five hundred organizations. Maxwell believed that influence was the main backbone of leadership, stating, "The true measure of leadership is influence – nothing more, nothing less."

The "law of influence" is one of Maxwell's identified twenty-one irrefutable laws of leadership. One example Maxwell uses in the case of influence is that of Princess Diana. Princess Diana convinced many people to rally to the causes of AIDS research, care for people with leprosy, and a ban on landmines. She also "influenced" the Clinton administration to support the ban on landmines.

Maxwell (1998) also reveals the "law of magnetism". He explains, "Who you get is not determined by what you want. It's determined by who you are," meaning that you will attract people just like you. The example he gives is with his ministry at Skyline Church. Skyline went from a church filled with musicians to a church filled with leaders. The reason was switching leaders. The previous leader was an excellent musician and Maxwell is an excellent leader. The "law of magnetism" explains that the musician attracted lots of musicians, and Maxwell being a leader attracted lots of leaders to Skyline.

The "law of magnetism" is a true principle, but it comes into conflict with the "law of influence". On the one hand, you have the belief that leaders can change people's motivation, desire, and actions. On the other hand, you have the belief that leaders attract people who already have the same motivation, desire, and actions. How does a leader influence people who already desire the same thing? Did Princess Diana influence thousands of people, or did she just attract people who already had the desire to help? How many times have we thought a person influenced hundreds of people to rally around a cause when, really, they were just able to attract those who were already interested? Was Princess Diana a leader because she influenced people, or because she was able to attract everyone who cared and aligned their support into efforts that could accomplish success? Maxwell shows the confusion that many experts on leadership experience with influence. They have bought into an idea that goes against other principles that seem true. Is the old age adage, "Birds of a feather flock together" really true?

Influence vs. Liberty

One of the major principles conflicting with influence is that of liberty and freedom. This is important because the foundation of the United States of America is based on the principle of liberty. Thomas Jefferson, one of the founding fathers, explained that liberty is an unalienable right. He states, in the Declaration of Independence, "We hold these truths to be self-evident, that all men are created equal, that they are endowed by their Creator with certain unalienable Rights, that among these are Life, Liberty and the pursuit of Happiness." The idea of influence is opposite of liberty. Liberty states that a person has the ability to act in accordance to his/her own desires and to the extent that it does not prevent another from doing the same. The idea of influence and control states that one person, through persuasion, charisma, or other tools and methods, can change another person from doing what he/she desires, to do something else.

Milton Friedman saw this to be true in the economic marketplace. He said, "So long as effective freedom of exchange is maintained, the central feature of the market organization of economic activity is that it prevents one person from interfering with another in respect of most of his activities... Indeed, a major source of objection to a free economy is precisely that it does this task so well. It gives people what they want instead of what a particular group thinks they ought to want. Underlying most arguments against the free market is a lack of belief in freedom itself." (Friedman, 2002) Milton Friedman understood that control and influence are opposite principles to freedom, and both principles cannot exist in the same environment. The foundation of America is based on principles of no-influence, so it is no surprise that the country was able to flourish and prosper. Over time, however, as America became more influence-oriented (controlling), its efficiency and power decreased.

Impact of No-Influence

On the surface, many do not realize the impact of the ideas of influence and no-influence. To understand the impact of the ideas, we will use *Key 5: Taking the Extreme*. Figure 15 below identifies the characteristics that come with the belief in each of the ideas. It identifies that those who believe their environment influences them do not take accountability for their lives, because they do not have full control over them. The idea of influence identifies that a person's environment is to blame for who a person is and what they do. This creates a control or be-controlled dichotomy. Most people would rather be in control than have another person controlling them, so they are more likely to be aggressive and try to influence others whenever possible.

"I create my environment"

More Likely to:
1. Plan things in advance
2. Be accountable
3. Have vision
4. Listen to others
5. Think of other people
6. Be at peace
7. Be organized

"My environment controls me"

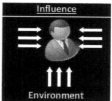

More Likely to:
1. Believe in luck and chance
2. Blame others
3. Be surprised
4. Be emotional
5. Try to control others
6. Feel controlled by others
7. Be reactive

Figure 15: No Influence & Influence Model (D. Kashiwagi, 2018)

The biggest issue with the belief in influence is that it makes the world more complex. There are millions of variables around us, and to understand what is occurring and why it is occurring, we would have to understand almost every variable. This is why many people feel that life is unpredictable— the impossibility of the human mind to comprehend and take in all the information. This creates a very unstable life that is filled with many unexpected events and circumstances, which causes people to become more emotional and reactive.

Believing in influence blinds the individual to the cause and effect of life. The individual never can understand why things are occurring, so it makes it seem that their environment and circumstances are random or by chance. This gives the person reason to not prepare or plan for the future because they do not know why things happen, and the future could easily be changed by other people or circumstances out of your control.

On the other hand, when a person believes there is no-influence, life becomes simpler. It becomes easier to foresee the future when you are the only one in control of it. Instead of needing to understand all the variables in life, the only thing you need to understand is yourself. This, of course, also causes people to take more accountability for their actions and look internally when things go wrong. Their life is more stable.

The biggest impact of influence comes when you look at how it affects relationships. It impacts everything in life dealing with people, such as:

1. Parent and child
2. Boss and worker
3. Friends and peers
4. Teacher and student
5. Husband and wife
6. Leader and followers
7. Buyer and seller

Most relationships operate under the premise of one person trying to influence another person. The parent and teacher are trying to mold the child to be and learn what they feel is important. The boss and leader are usually trying to influence the follower and worker to improve their performance and value. The seller tries to motivate and influence the buyer to want their product, and spouses try to shape each other to meet their expectations and desires.

The most important impact of the influence idea is that it causes people to try to communicate more or, in other words, talk. The main reason to communicate or talk is to try to influence the ideas, actions, and understanding of other people. When you feel that you cannot influence people and people control their own lives, then in most instances there is no reason to communicate anymore. You will begin to talk less and listen more.

No Influence Leadership: Summary

The ability to know the truth is the ability to accurately see reality. The more accurately we understand reality, the more successful we become. The less resistance that we run into, the less pain we experience in life, and the happier we become.

Learning to identify truth is the single most important skill a person can develop when they are young. It not only brings wealth, but it brings happiness. It enables a person to do more in their life by making it simpler and clearer.

The less someone understands, the more options they think are possible. The more options you think are possible, the more confusing life becomes, which prevents you from being able to do anything. Barry Schwartz, a famous psychologist, identified that seeing multiple options paralyzes a person (Schwartz, 2004). When people see many choices that they could make, and they have no way of knowing which choice is the best, it causes fear. This is because the more options you have, the greater your risk of picking an option that does not have the most optimal outcome. When people can't clearly see the best option, it leads them to inaction.

The more we understand about reality, the more accurate expectations we will have in life, and the less options we will see. Understanding reality enables us to move from one moment in life to another with quicker speed and less regret. As you begin to see reality more accurately, it will also allow you to see further ahead in your life. It will minimize your fear and worry. You will have less times in your life that you are surprised, and it will enable you to be more stable and at peace with life.

Hopefully, as you learn to use the five keys that unlock the truth, you will better understand life and yourself.

"Many people, especially ignorant people, want to punish you for speaking the truth, for being correct, for being you. Never apologize for being correct, or for being years ahead of your time. If you're right and you know it, speak your mind. Speak your mind. Even if you are a minority of one, the truth is still the truth."

— Mahatma Gandhi

Bibliography

Allen, James (2012). As a man thinketh. Penguin.

Andrews, Jane Anne (1994). "Applying Deming's philosophy and principles to the instructional process in higher education " Retrospective Theses and Dissertations.

American Psychology Association (APA) (September, 2017). "By the numbers: Stress on campus".

Beauchamp, S. (April 3rd, 2017). New data from Cambridge Mobile Telematics shows distracted driving dangers. Cambridge Mobile Telematics.

Biography.com (February 15, 2018), Morgan Freeman. A&E Television Networks.

Biography.com (February 15, 2018), Warren Buffett Biography. A&E Television Networks.

Davis, Rebecca. "The Doctor Who Championed Hand-Washing and Briefly Saved Lives", NPR, Morning Edition. January 12, 2015.

Dylan, Bob. "Blowing in the Wind." The Freewheelin' Bob Dylan, Warner/Chappell Music, Blossom Music, Kinney Music Ltd., M. Witmark & Sons & Warner (Music Label), 1963, track 1.

Einstein, Albert – Biographical (2014). Nobelprize.org. Nobel Media AB.

Einstein, Albert (December 25th, 1919). Induction and Deduction in Physics(pp108). Berliner Tageblatt.

Eliot, T.S (1934). "Choruses from The Rock. (pp127)," New York: Harcourt, Brace & World.

Flansburg, Scott (Sep 8th, 2012), The Human Calculator® Scott Flansburg on Guinness World Records TV in the United Kingdom

Garcia-Pelayo, Gonzalo (2017). "Gonzalo Garcia-Pelayo"

Gillett, Rachel (2015). "11 wildly successful people who dropped out of high school." Business Insider.

Gladwell, Malcolm (2008). Outliers: the story of success. New York:Little, Brown and Co.

Gray (2006). The Bob Dylan Encyclopedia, (pp. 64). New York: Continuum.

Hawking, Stephen (1942). A Brief History of Time. New York: Bantam Books.

Hevesi, Dennis. (Jan 8th, 2007) "Momofuku Ando, 96, Dies; Invented Instant Ramen.", The New York Times.

History.com Staff (2009). "Henry Ford." History.com, A&E Television Networks.

History.com staff (2009), Christopher Columbus, A+E Network.

Kashiwagi, D. (2018). How to Know Everything Without Knowing Anything Vol.1", Performance Based Studies Research Group, Mesa, AZ. Publisher: KSM Inc., 2018.

Kashiwagi, D. (2018). How to Know Everything Without Knowing Anything Vol.2", Performance Based Studies Research Group, Mesa, AZ. Publisher: KSM Inc., 2018.

Kashiwagi, Jacob. Leadership is alignment not influence. Diss. Arizona State University, 2007.

Keller, Bill (Dec 5. 2013). "Nelson Mandela, South Africa's Liberator as Prisoner and President, Dies at 95." The New York Times.

"La fabulosa historia de Los Pelayos" (noviembre de 2003). Blog Entry, Microsiervos.

Lee, Bruce (1987). Chinese Gung Fu: The Philosophical Art of Self Defense (pp11). Black Belt Communications.

Lee, Bruce (Sep 1, 2015). Bruce Lee Striking Thoughts: Bruce Lee's Wisdom for Daily Living (Bruce Lee Library). Tuttle Publishing.

Lee, Bruce (Sep 8, 2015). Bruce Lee The Tao of Gung Fu: A Study in the Way of Chinese Martial Art (pp. 114). Tuttle Publishing

Popova, Maria (2018), Be Like Water: The Philosophy and Origin of Bruce Lee's Famous Metaphor for Resilience, Brainpicking.

Merrill, Douglas (26 Sept. 2012). "Why Multitasking Doesn't Work." Forbes, Forbes Magazine.

Friedman, Milton (1962). Capitalism and Freedom(p371). The University of Chicago.

My Yellowstone Park. "Wolves in Yellowstone National Park." (May 22nd, 2017,)

Plato, Rowe, C., Plato., Plato., Plato. and Plato. (2010). The last days of Socrates. London: Penguin Books.

Rolling Stone. "500 Greatest Songs of All Time." (Apr 7th, 2011).

Snijders, C., Tazelaar, F., and Batenburg, R. (2003) Electronic decision support for procurement management: evidence on whether computers can make better procurement decisions. Journal of Purchasing and Supply Management, 9 (2003) 191-198.

Sadie, Stanley (Apr 19th, 2017). "Wolfgang Amadeus Mozart." Encyclopædia Britannica,

Schwartz, Barry (2004)."The paradox of choice.", TED: Ideas worth spreading.

Sinek, Simon (2011). Start with why: How great leaders inspire everyone to take action. Penguin.

Stevens, Hampton (June 24, 2010). "Michael Jackson's Unparalleled Influence." The Atlantic.

Urist, Jacoba (Sept 24th. 2014). "What the Marshmallow Test Really Teaches About Self-Control." The Atlantic,

Wilberforce, William (2018). Christian History

Thanks for Reading!

Here's access to
TWO FREE LESSONS
from our online
course!

LeadAZ.org/Success

Who Is Jacob Kashiwagi?

Dr. Jacob Kashiwagi is a thought leader in leadership development, procurement, project management, and supply chain management. He co-developed the Best Value Approach through a 26-year global research effort. This groundbreaking model is the most licensed technology at Arizona State University in the past 20 years (61 licenses) and has been tested on over 2,000 projects valued over $2 billion, with a 98% success rating (on time, within budget, and client highly satisfied), and savings of 10-30% on all project costs.

The global success of the Best Value Approach inspired Dr. Jacob to author the No-Influence Leadership Model, a radical approach to teaching leadership skills to students and professionals. This unique methodology empathizes that effective leadership is about understanding and aligning expertise without attempting to change or influence others. Dr. Jacob has taught this approach to over 8,000 management professionals, 1,500 college students, and 1,200 high school students. He has personally mentored over 150 students helping them use the No-Influence to develop lucrative careers and overcome personal instability (substance abuse, family trauma, depression, severe anxiety etc.)

Today, Dr. Jacob continues to champion programs to advance the field of leadership development. He is the Managing Director at Kashiwagi Solution Model Inc., a Best Value Consultant at Performance Based Studies Research Group, and the Chairman of the Board at Leadership Society of Arizona a non-profit educational research and program development organization that specializes in leadership and social-emotional learning.

You can book Dr. Jacob or Dr. Dean for speaking and keynote events by visiting:

LeadAZ.org/speaking

Want to Learn More?

Leadership Society of Arizona (LSA) is a non-profit educational research and program development organization that specializes in leadership and social-emotional learning. LSA uses the leadership methods taught in this book to help revolutionize the education system. LSA programs teach students unique skills to help them become more rational thinkers and problem solvers. Through 40 programs at 17 schools with over 1,200 students report that 75% of them feel less stressed and 64% feel more confident about their futures.

This book was published as a joint-effort between LSA, KSM inc., and PBSRG. Here are some of the services they offer:
- Teacher Training
- Student Coaching
- Professional Life Coaching
- Supply Chain & Procurement Services
- Education System Optimization (high schools and districts)
- Performance Analysis and Consultation

For a FREE Consultation Call Visit:
LeadAZ.org/contact-us